when kids
hurt

when kids hurt

hurt

HELP FOR ADULTS NAVIGATING THE ADOLESCENT MAZE

CHAP CLARK
AND STEVE RABEY

BakerBooks

a division of Baker Publishing Group
Grand Rapids, Michigan

Published by Baker Books
a division of Baker Publishing Group
P.O. Box 6287, Grand Rapids, MI 49516-6287
www.bakerbooks.com

Printed in the United States of America

Library of Congress Cataloging-in-Publication Data
Clark, Chap, 1954–
    When kids hurt : help for adults navigating the adolescent maze / Chap
    Clark and Steve Rabey.
        p.   cm.
    Includes bibliographical references.
    ISBN 978-0-8010-7183-6 (pbk.)
    1. Teenagers—United States—Social conditions. 2. Teenagers—United
States—Attitudes. 3. Adolescent psychology—United States. I. Rabey, Steve.
II. Title.
HQ796.C555 2009
305.235′50973—dc22   2009000367

contents

introduction

my excellent adventure

In the 1989 movie *Bill & Ted's Excellent Adventure*, Keanu Reeves plays Ted Logan, a California high school student who cares more about rock music than his American history class, which is the reason he is about to fail the class. If he doesn't shape up, his authoritarian father says he will send Ted to the Alaskan Military Academy.

Thankfully, a guru named Rufus appears from the year 2688. Rufus (played by George Carlin) takes Ted and fellow slacker Bill on a guided tour of the past where the two students meet historical figures whose names they repeatedly mispronounce: Socrates becomes "So-Crates," Sigmund Freud is pronounced "Frood," while Ludwig van Beethoven becomes "Beeth Oven."

Still, when all is said and done, Bill and Ted's oral report gets an A+. An excellent adventure, indeed!

Recently I had an adventure of my own, but mine wasn't a journey into the past.

Into Foreign Territory

Hillary had his Everest, Cousteau his oceans, and Lewis and Clark their journey of exploration. So where did I go?

I spent more than six months working as a substitute teacher at a public high school in north Los Angeles County. I chose Crescenta Valley High School, a nationally recognized Blue Ribbon School for excellence in academic achievement, because of its diverse ethnic student body; its strong programs in sports, music, and drama; and its middle-class socioeconomic status (there's a big disparity in how much students' parents earn, but none are filthy rich or desperately poor).

Plus, the school's administration was supportive, so long as I agreed to focus first on my duties as a teacher, not harass kids, and not reveal identifying information about the kids who invited me into their lives. (That's why all the names have been changed, but all quotes come from real students.)

I spend a lot of time in academic circles where scholars debate competing theories of adolescent development, but the goal of my excellent adventure was to move beyond theory to observation, so I could understand more fully what life is like for middle adolescents. In academic terms, I was conducting participant-observation research to create an ethnographic study of a specific population: today's teens.

For more than six months I spent nearly every day with high school students as a participant-observer in their world. I wanted to get close and to listen to them, to develop enough trust for them to let me in to places that few adults are allowed. I wanted to discern their complex, contradictory worldviews and watch how they navigate the multilayered expectations and relationships that control their landscape.

Within a few weeks of my arrival at the school, students warmed up to me so thoroughly they were soon being surprisingly candid with me (and sometimes embarrassingly so) about their lives.

By the time my six months in the school were over, I had received hundreds of notes, songs, poems, and scribbled letters that kids handed to me as I walked the halls or entered a classroom. Most of the time these messages came from students I couldn't quite place and had never interacted with in any deep or significant way.

In my vain and silly moments I told myself that young people naturally trust me more than they do most adults. But in my saner moments I have come to a more sobering realization: my expressions of sincerity and concern—no matter how fleeting or superficial—served to open the door to young people who were desperate to talk to *any* safe adult about their lives.

I conducted twelve scientifically designed focus groups with carefully selected groups of high school juniors and seniors (ten in the United States and two in Canada). Plus, I surveyed most of the significant literature and research on youth culture and teen development.

I was amazed by what I found. While I can't say that anything surprised me totally, I was repeatedly reminded of how little those of us who raise kids or work with them really know about the inner lives of midadolescents.

After that experience I wrote my 2004 book, *Hurt: Inside the World of Today's Teenagers*, so adults could learn to become more astute students of the kids we are responsible to nurture.

Mixed Reactions

When I told people about my adventure, both students and adults wondered if I had lost my mind. "Why would anyone want to study us?" asked Sharon, a seventeen-year-old high school junior. "I mean, what's the big deal about kids?"

Sharon had been bugging me for some time about my motive for hanging around the school. My explanation that I was taking a sabbatical leave from my teaching job at Fuller Theological Seminary failed to satisfy her, as did my lighthearted quips about liking kids, or my more serious explanation that I believed most adults had little understanding of where adolescents were coming from.

Sharon suspected an ulterior motive and worried that talking to me would be threatening to her friends. "Is this going to make you famous?" she asked.

I laughed out loud. "After writing some books that few actually read," I said, "I gave up on fame a long time ago."

"Then, why?" she said. "Why are you doing this? Will it really matter to anyone?"

Frankly, I shared her concern, as did Jake, a junior.

"Tell them our story," he remarked. "Tell them the truth—that nobody cares, that nobody listens, that teachers and coaches and cops and parents don't even know who we are. Tell them that and see if anybody listens. Ha! Not a chance!"

As a parent of three kids and as someone who has devoted my entire professional life to "youth work," I feared Sharon and Jake were right. I had spent hundreds of hours gathering valuable insights into today's kids. But would anybody care? Would all my work make any difference?

From *Hurt* to *When Kids Hurt*

Nearly two hundred thousand books are published in America every year, and fewer than 5 percent of them ever sell five thousand copies. The numbers are even worse for academic books (*Hurt* was published by Baker Academic, an imprint of Baker Publishing Group). But *Hurt* beat the odds, connecting with readers in a powerful way and selling nearly fifty thousand copies, which is an astounding number for a scholarly book about kids.

Over the next few years after writing the book, as I talked to parents, taught students at Fuller Seminary, or spoke to youth workers (one by one or thousands at a time), it seemed that everyone had questions for me about *Hurt*:

Were those real kids?

Did those kids really say all those things?

And what can we do about the things you told us?

My typical answers were:

Yes.

Yes.

And that's an excellent question!

It's my desire to answer that third question that has led to the new book you now hold in your hands.

In addition to talking with parents, students, and youth workers, I had many long talks with Robert Hosack, my intrepid editor at Baker. Robert is a man who loves books and believes they can impact people's lives. People had been asking Robert about *Hurt* too, and he convinced me to consider creating a book that was less academic in tone and more practical in its application. The results of that process are found in *When Kids Hurt*.

Robert and I decided to ask Steve Rabey, a veteran writer who works with me to edit the magazine *YouthWorker Journal* (youth worker.com), to help make the transition from *Hurt* into *When Kids Hurt*.

I did not go back to high school for more observation, but Steve and I reviewed and critiqued everything I had written before, changing and updating those things that needed tweaking. (To see if and how I changed my mind about anything, see the conclusion of this book.)

We also added updated info about trends in youth culture, many of these written by Paul Asay, who writes the "Youth Culture Update" department in *YouthWorker Journal*.

Finally, I invited dozens of respected peers in academia and youth work to contribute their insights to this project. Nearly forty of them accepted my offer to write their responses and observations. In many cases, these mini-essays help answer some of the "so what?" questions readers had been asking me over the years about how to apply the lessons of *Hurt*.

Now What?

Like *Hurt*, my new effort, *When Kids Hurt*, attempts to help adults understand kids and move toward them in ways that can help them grow and become the kinds of adults our world needs to survive and thrive.

Those of you who read *Hurt* should find some familiar ideas along with some new information. Hopefully, all of it will be easier to digest and apply. And for those of you who did not read *Hurt*, let me welcome you to a journey that began years ago in a school far, far away! (If after reading *When Kids Hurt*, you want more background information, research, and footnotes, you might benefit from reading *Hurt* too.)

And as I worked on this new project, once again, I could hear the voice of Sharon, the high school student who asked me: "Is this going to make you famous?"

11

Here's how I would respond to Sharon today: "No, Sharon, I don't think this book will get me on Oprah's show or *The Daily Show*, but if I can help adults understand amazing, wonderful people like you and be more loving and helpful in the ways they relate to you, that would make it all worthwhile."

It is my hope and prayer that *When Kids Hurt* can help you on your very own excellent adventure with the young men and women in your world.

part 1

kids' brave new world

1

the changing face of adolescence

Kids can be fun, as anyone who has raised them or works with them knows. At times they seem so carefree and joyful that they're great to be around. Their optimism about the future and their limitless potential are amazing. And their social lives—full of dances, games, events, concerts—are a whirlwind of activity.

Many adults who look at the world of today's kids feel a sense of continuity between what's happening now and their own happy growing-up years.

But there's another, darker side of the teen years. While some kids look forward to a bright future, others wrestle with fears, loneliness, and insecurities. They long for something deeper than the shallow friendships that surround them. They dream of a culture in which their worth is measured by more than external factors, such as attractiveness, performance, or image.

These are the two perspectives that emerge when adults enter the world of today's teens. Either contemporary adolescents are highly nurtured, motivated, and functioning or they are in dire straits.

In a sense, both perspectives are valid and real. It is true that many adolescents appear genuinely happy, carefree, and seemingly healthy. But in this book I want to go beneath the surface, as I did with the students I got to know during my journey.

Time and time again I was amazed to see how kids who typically projected a positive image painted a much different picture when we talked one-on-one and they opened up about their deepest concerns.

Two Schools of Thought on Teens

Twenty-five centuries ago the Greek philosopher Socrates complained about the youth of his day. Or did he? Here's the quote that many speakers and preachers have circulated:

> Our youth love luxury. They have bad manners, contempt for authority; they show disrespect for their elders, and love to chatter in places of exercise. Children are now tyrants, not the servants of their household. They no longer rise when their elders enter the room. They contradict their parents, chatter before company, gobble up their food, and tyrannize their teachers.

Actually, Socrates never said any such thing. But people still repeat the "quote" because it supports their view that problems youth face haven't changed much over the centuries.

Some eight centuries after Socrates, St. Augustine described his own teen years in his *Confessions*. The situation he describes is instantly recognizable in our own day, suggesting that things haven't really changed that much: "I had a period of leisure, living at home

Youth Culture Update

Juvenile Behavior

Kids today are more violent than ever.

Police in cities nationwide are seeing big jumps in violent crimes perpetrated by juveniles. In Boston, weapons crimes involving children under age eighteen shot up 103 percent. Experts say communities are spending less on cops and child welfare programs these days. Gang leaders are also getting out of prison, reclaiming old turf and drafting new youngsters into the drug trade.

with my parents and not doing any work at all, the brambles of lust grew up right over my head."

Today an adult arguing for the "stable" side of how young people are doing might state the argument like this: Kids have always been kids. Things may change on the surface, but teenagers have always been with us and have always pushed the extremes of adult society. They are basically the same now as they were thousands of years ago. Only the styles have changed.

These adults might even connect the dots between adolescent icons, such as:

- James Dean, the sulking antihero of the 1955 film *Rebel without a Cause*
- Eddie Haskell, who was the central character in TV's *Leave It to Beaver* in the 1950s and 1960s
- Arthur Fonzarelli (a.k.a. the Fonz) from *Happy Days* in the 1970s and 1980s
- Bart Simpson, lead brat of the animated show *The Simpsons*, which debuted in 1989 and is still going strong two decades later

In a sense, the debate about whether or not adolescence is changing is like a big Rorschach inkblot test. People see what they want to see.

So, where do I land in this debate? Do I think the world of young people is the same as it always has been? Or do I think things have changed in significant and worrisome ways? Sign me up for "significant" and "worrisome."

In the pages that follow, I will argue that adolescence is a fundamentally different thing today than it was thirty years ago (when many of today's Boomer parents were growing up) or a century ago, when people first started using the term *adolescence*.

Before then, people generally spoke about two primary stages of the human lifespan: childhood and adulthood. Once a child had successfully mastered the rituals, rites of passage, and training necessary to be accepted into the adult community, he or she was assimilated as a full member of that community.

Now we all accept the reality of a "middle" period between childhood and adulthood. In fact, our word for adolescence comes from a Latin word that means "to grow."

Increasingly, many social thinkers are using a new term—*midadolescence*—to describe the changing world of today's teens. As they see it, midadolescence is a period when teens are forced to function as several distinct selves in their distinct social worlds. To survive, a young person must learn how to be a child, a student, an athlete/musician/video gamer, and a friend, while also continuing the ever-lengthening process of determining who he or she is.

As our understanding of teens has continued to grow, the emergence of this new stage of life known as midadolescence shows that the world of teens is changing, bringing with it new and at times very difficult challenges for both kids and the adults in their lives.

At the same time, observers are now describing a new phase known as "emerging adulthood" in which people in their twenties and thirties continue to delay some of the experiences that once symbolized adulthood, such as living on their own, marrying, or figuring out what they want to do with their lives.

An article in *USA Today* summarized "emerging adulthood" as follows: "Once upon a time, 18- to 25-year-olds were considered adults. That's a fairy tale now, say most parents of college students, and their kids agree in a new study that confirms 'growing up' comes later."

Some researchers believe that in recent decades culture has changed so quickly that the developmental, societal, and relational needs of children have been neglected. As a result, by the time children reach adolescence, they have been left on their own to attempt to navigate their path toward adulthood through obstacles like shifts in cultural values and structure, changes in the form of family, and the challenges of peer relations, gender, ethnic uniqueness, morality, character, and ethics.

Regardless of whether you're in the "stable" school or the "changing" school, I hope that, as you read this book and as you work with kids, you will keep your eyes and ears open to the signs of transformation in the world of today's teens. Like many other adults, I believe that there is something different going on today,

18

▬▬ *Scarce Sleep* ▬▬

Teens today are wired—in more ways than one. According to a study by the National Sleep Foundation, teens that have lots of electronic gear in their rooms are twice as likely to fall asleep in school. The study found that almost all children in grades 6–12 had at least one electronic gadget—be it a computer, cell phone, television, or some other device—in their bedrooms. Thirty-nine percent had four or more.

and these changes create new challenges, issues, and dilemmas for adolescents.

Coming to Terms

How would you define the word *adolescent*? Here's what one teacher told me when I asked her: "The opaque glance and the pimples. The fancy new nakedness they're all dressed up in with no place to go. The eyes full of secrets they have a strong hunch everybody is on to. The shadowed brow. Being not quite a child and not quite a grown-up either is hard work, and they look it. Living in two worlds at once is no picnic."

Developmental theorists would define it like this: Adolescence is not a blend of both child and adult, nor is it an expanded phase of either. Adolescence is a unique phase of life that must be understood and dealt with on its own merits.

Developmental psychologist John Santrock went further, saying: ". . . defining when adolescence ends is not an easy task. It has been said that adolescence begins in biology and ends in culture."

I've spent time with both the experts and the kids, and here's what I have concluded: Adolescence is a period in which young people engage in a psychosocial, independent search for a unique identity or separateness. The goal of this search is a certain knowledge of who one is in relation to others, a willingness to take responsibility for who one is becoming, and a realized commitment to live with others in community.

The Timing and Duration of Adolescence

If it's difficult to define adolescence, it is even tougher to define its parameters—when it begins and ends. While we might like a clear-cut definition, the comments of social scientists are ambiguous. No one really knows!

Many experts say the beginning point of adolescence is puberty. But these same experts debate when the exact physiological changes of puberty begin. And these changes are even more difficult to detect in boys than in girls, for whom the age of puberty has been slowly dropping for more than a century, to as early as eleven years of age.

It is even more difficult to determine when adolescence ends. Almost no social scientists or developmental theorists use legal age as a reference point for the end of adolescence. That's because the process of growing up is more than an accumulation of years. It is the process of individuation. It involves psychosocial and chronological factors, such as readiness for marriage, as well as legal factors, which vary from country to country, on such issues as when citizens are old enough to drive a car, smoke cigarettes, drink alcoholic beverages, or vote in elections.

When culture affirms that someone has individuated in terms of identity, is willing to take responsibility for his or her life and choices, and has entered interdependently into the community and adult relationships, that person is said to be an adult. This is the true end point of adolescence, and it typically comes somewhere in the middle to late twenties.

What Has Changed?

Those adults who see something new and different in today's adolescents wonder what has changed. Is it the content or impact of media? Is it the limited attention spans of today's harried parents? Is it changes in our educational systems? Is it a lack of religious conviction or a loss of family values?

When I go in search of what happened and when, I turn my gaze back to the 1960s and the massive social upheavals that altered the landscape of all segments of American society.

Youth were at the center of the '60s, and many of the most significant changes of this period altered many of our culture's systems, structures, organizations, and institutions that had been designed to nurture and care for the young.

During the 1960s, and even the 1950s, adolescents enjoyed an unprecedented status in the dominant culture. There was an identifiable youth "subculture" that was sometimes referred to as the "teenage culture." And as the concerns and passions of this adolescent subculture were articulated by recording artists like Elvis Presley or the Beatles and portrayed in movies such as *Rebel without a Cause*, there was a growing industry of entertainment companies and clothing companies that focused ever more attention on meeting the youth culture's needs (and collecting its many dollars!).

The 1960s was a turbulent period, however, and saw a marked increase in social unrest and global upheaval. The headlines of the period (escalation of the Cold War, potential global nuclear exchanges, the Vietnam War, racism and the battle for civil rights) showed the underbelly of an American national narrative that was painful for everyone. Meanwhile, the assassination of powerful public figures (John F. Kennedy, Martin Luther King Jr., Robert Kennedy) revealed

Youth Culture Update

Get a Job

According to some experts, youth are increasingly bypassing traditional summertime jobs, like being a lifeguard, selling hot dogs at baseball games, or working at state and national parks, in favor of internships that will look good on résumés later on.

"I think the desire for summer jobs has changed a little bit," said Howard Feldstein, director for the Arlington Employment Center near Washington, D.C. "Kids are looking not only for income, but what makes them look good for the next step in their life."

21

our vulnerability as well as that of our heroes, while shattering our sense of social cohesion. In a sense, our nation lost its childhood and innocence during those difficult years. At the same time, teens felt acutely the uncertainties that surrounded them.

These were dark and frightening days for all Americans, and a tremendous sense of confusion, societal insecurity, and cultural instability spilled into nearly every institution, social structure, and relationship in the nation. The "good old days" of the 1950s were over (debate continues about whether they had ever really existed!).

The 1970s saw the Watergate scandal, which only furthered our society's distrust in its established leaders. By the mid-1970s, many people had accepted a social philosophy that was summarized in some of the era's main mottoes:

"Live and let live."
"If it feels good, do it."
"Looking out for number 1."

Assessing the Damage

Looking back on this period from the distance of four decades, we can see that the biggest change affecting adolescents was the shift in the focus of adults and our social systems and institutions. Until the 1960s, many adults and their institutions had focused on caring for young people through such efforts as youth sports, religious training, and outdoor activities. But as we emerged from the 1960s, many adults began trying to find a safe place or haven of security and rest *for themselves*. As adults waged a fight for their own emotional and relational survival, children got the time and attention that was left over, which was not much.

As a result, our society was transformed. Adults went from being part of a relatively stable and cohesive community intent on caring for its young to a free-for-all of independent and fragmented people seeking their own pleasure and survival. At this point many adolescents found themselves in a deepening hole of systemic rejection or abandonment by the adults they had once been able to look up to and trust.

No #$*@

Experts say that today's children might put the vocabulary of drunken sailors to the test. The average adolescent uses somewhere between eighty or ninety cuss words every day, according to researcher Timothy Jay—described by the *Sacramento Bee* as "one of the leading scholars on cursing in the United States."

That's more profane than kids have been in the past, and Jay, a professor at the Massachusetts College of Liberal Arts, suggests that television and the Internet are helping youngsters feel more comfortable with swearing. But parents wield the biggest influence, and he adds that cursing is a natural part of growing up. "It starts as soon as they learn how to talk," he says. "At a young age, they're attentive to emotions. When you're swearing to be funny or when you're angry—that just draws them right to it."

One of the most striking aspects of this transformation occurred within the structure of the family itself, as sociologist David Elkind explained in his 1994 book *Ties That Stress: The New Family Imbalance.*

Elkind says that during the post–World War II golden era, men in America enjoyed stable, routinized family lives; children and adolescents were nurtured and cared for. All this stability and nurture depended on women, who adapted to varied roles and expectations and assumed significant responsibility for other family members' happiness, often at the expense of their own.

But as the culture virtually dismantled its previously rigid guidelines for family life, a new family imbalance occurred as men and women attempted to redefine their roles and relationships within the family system. The consequence of this imbalance fell on the children, who were left to fend for themselves as their parents became preoccupied with finding their own way in life.

So how did all these cultural changes impact kids? First, the definition of *family* was radically altered from the institutional longevity of "two or more persons related by birth, marriage, or adoption who reside in the same household," as defined by the Census Bureau in 1990, to the current definition of a free-flowing, organic "commitment" between people who love each other.

This change is exemplified in a Tufts University course for undergraduates titled "Family and Intimate Relationships," in which family is "defined broadly as those with whom one shares resources and values and to whom one has a long-term commitment."

The second change was in how we view the institution of the family. We moved from a culture with a divorce rate that affected 2 percent of the married population (in 1940) to a society in which 43 percent of first-time marriages end in separation or divorce within fifteen years of marriage (as of 2002).

I observed the impact of divorce firsthand while attending a dance competition in Orlando with my daughter. Of the thirteen girls on the team, all from the high school where I spent my time substitute teaching, more than half came from divorced families. Of the parents who attended:

- One forty-year-old mother brought her sixty-seven-year-old live-in boyfriend.
- One fifty-six-year-old father was accompanied by his thirty-one-year-old girlfriend.

Youth Culture Update

Self-Injury on Rise

Nearly half of high school students have engaged in non-suicidal, self-injuring behavior more than once the previous year, according to a study published recently in *Psychological Medicine*.

According to the study, behavior includes things like pulling out hair or pushing things underneath their own fingernails. But 28 percent of students between ninth and twelfth grade said they'd gone to even greater lengths to hurt themselves, including cutting, burning, and self-tattooing. White teens were more likely to engage in such behaviors than African American teens.

- The fifty-six-year-old father's ex-wife was accompanied by her current live-in boyfriend.

It is indeed a brave new world when it comes to what the word *family* means.

For the adolescent who is trying to hold on to something—anything—that is stable and safe, such societal changes affecting divorce, adult sexuality, and cohabitation have had a strong, destabilizing effect.

Allowing for the definition of family to be reshaped to line up with almost any casual encounter between two or more people is to deny thousands of years of societal history. The adolescent is left to discern how to handle the many conflicting messages related to home, stable relationships, and internal security—all while trying to figure out how to survive lengthened adolescence. This only adds to the aloneness most kids feel.

From Adolescence to Midadolescence

We could see the consequences of the 1960s in the early 1980s. Young people were maturing at different rates, depending on the stability and dependability of their families. Age had less to do with it than experience. And by the 1990s, a newly named stage known as midadolescence emerged as a distinct phase of development.

An e-newsletter from the American Counseling Association defined midadolescence as follows:

Midadolescence generally corresponds to grades 9 through 12 and ages 15 through 18. Many of the developmental changes of early adolescence are extended and refined during midadolescence. This period also presents new challenges and changes for high school students. . . . As students move through high school, they are progressively faced with important decisions regarding future schooling, career paths, and related options. This is both exciting and stressful for many adolescents. The exhilaration of new opportunities and freedoms is often coupled with a sense of isolation and vulnerability ("What if I make the wrong choice?"). Adolescents "face leaving the world that they have always known and stepping out on their own." . . . Increased privileges, such as driving a car and scheduling one's own time, also represent

25

Movies Tell the Truth about Today's Teen Culture

Craig Detweiler

Chap Clark's research convinced me that adolescence starts earlier and lasts longer than I had thought. We see this happen physically with issues of puberty. Teens aspiring to abstinence before marriage are in for a long struggle (or an early marriage!). But prolonged adolescence also raises huge issues of responsibility. Delayed decision making pushes adolescence from high school or college into graduate school. At Fuller Seminary my grad students are still sorting out their calling. Some are paying their bills for the first time. Others are covered by their parents' largesse even into their thirties!

What music or movies might reflect the stats explored in *When Kids Hurt*? The three stages of adolescence outlined by Chap Clark are contained within the movie title *13 Going on 30*. While the film plays as a romantic comedy, the issues behind it are decidedly adult. Are teens growing up too fast, facing adult pressures before they are equipped to handle them? How many teenagers feel like Tom Hanks in *Big*? They are like children, forced to navigate a world well beyond their level of maturity. We see teens trading places with their parents in *Freaky Friday*. While adults evade responsibility, teens take on adult roles far too soon.

Movies may also offer false assurances in chaste films like *A Walk to Remember*, *The Princess Diaries,* and *High School Musical*. Parents are comforted by sanitized images of good kids making smart lifestyle choices. But the success of these safe films may mask the truth of teen behavior, residing several layers below glossy Hollywood surfaces.

In the real world Anne Hathaway followed *The Princess Diaries* by playing *Havoc* with her career. In *Havoc* two suburban teens dive into the inner city in search of decidedly cheap thrills. It is one long, bad trip. While Zac Effron and Vanessa Hudgens were act-

increased responsibilities. Freedom and responsibility represent two sides of a developmental coin that can become a major source of conflict between high school students and their caregivers.

In this book I want to help you understand and address the changing face of adolescence. There are three main reasons you need to grasp these changes.

Newfound Freedoms of Midadolescents

First, most of the newfound freedoms that accompany midadolescence were originally granted in late adolescence (and even twenty

ing innocent in *High School Musical*, they were taking alluring photos of each other offscreen. Vanessa's soft porn pictures were plastered across the Internet. The hidden side of teen life slipped out despite the Disney marketing machine.

Crazy/Beautiful was written as a tough, R-rated drama about good girls gone bad. It shows a tolerant parent allowing a daughter free rein with damaging results. As the "crazy" part of the movie, it turns out that Nicole (Kirsten Dunst) didn't want unchecked freedom. She longed for a loving structure. The studio softened *Crazy/Beautiful*, turning a cautionary prodigal daughter story into a PG-13 romance. Layers of teen misbehavior were literally covered up.

Smarter, independent films expose the gap between adult perceptions and teen realities. *Brick* depicts an adolescent underworld hidden from affluent parents. It places a private eye story inside a high school, with nary a caring adult in sight. The cult classic *Donnie Darko* searches for solutions beyond Ritalin. Along with characters in *Garden State* and *The Chumscrubber*, Donnie throws away the meds, choosing to feel bad rather than feel nothing. *Donnie Darko* rewards repeat viewings; what appears to mock Christianity turns into a surprising savior story.

Youth workers and parents will find plenty of scary, hard-hitting scenes of adolescent life in *Thirteen*. Co-written by teen actor Nikki Reed, *Thirteen* demonstrates what happens when adults are too busy to pay attention to their kids. Even "good" girls can sink into petty crime and self-abuse as a desperate cry for help. *Thirteen* illustrates how and why a tragedy like *The Virgin Suicides* arises. While parents linger downstairs, a separate teen universe unravels upstairs.

For those tempted to dismiss movies as mere fiction, documentaries allow teens to tell their stories. In *Chain Camera* students pass along a video camera from person to person over the course of a school year. They invite viewers into their bedrooms and

years ago fifteen- and sixteen-year-olds were characteristically late adolescents). The freedom that comes with the privilege to drive, for example, presents an opportunity to get away from the perceived confines of parental authority, to spend additional time with peers, and to find new avenues of discovery, adventure, and even risk.

This freedom used to be reserved for late adolescents who were close to completing the adolescent journey and who were better equipped to handle the consequences of freedom. But things may not work so well when this freedom is granted to midadolescents who retain the residue of self-centered childhood and may not have the developmental acumen to make the kind of choices that are required

private lives. *American Teen* follows four students in rural Indiana. At first, the teens conform to our stereotypes about jocks and cheerleaders. But by the conclusion of the film, we discover what is missing in the students' lives—no adults are involved at a deep level of friendship or mentorship. These teens are broken by the absence of caring adults.

How do we develop disciples of Christ among our young people, given the demands of contemporary culture? It takes time to get below the surface with teens. Ministries must invest in their junior and senior high programs, pouring even more resources into youth ministries staff and volunteers. Late adolescence, the twenties, is when transformation takes place. And this may be the age of youth ministry staff. Give staff plenty of opportunities to attend conferences, get training, and engage in seminary education while they serve students. While leaders are molding midadolescents, they're actually maturing into their own adulthood.

The Lilly Endowment created a program to introduce high school leaders to seminary education. Chap Clark directed the Student Leadership Program for Young Life students at Fuller Seminary. As a professor, I understood that I was teaching midadolescents. I adjusted the academic demands accordingly. Time will tell how the students will respond, but the program ended up having the most immediate impact on the leaders chaperoning the high school students. The multivalent thinking necessary in grad school was best directed at the leaders who were guiding the kids! Churches and youth workers must recognize that we are all in process, both leaders and students. While our hired help takes cares of our students, the greatest growth may be solidifying in our late adolescent leaders.

Craig Detweiler directs the Reel Spirituality Institute at Fuller Theological Seminary. His feature documentary, *Purple State of Mind*, bridges the religious and cultural gulf in America. Craig's latest book is *Into the Dark: Seeing the Sacred in 21st-Century Cinema* (Baker Academic, 2007).

to navigate an automobile. (This is the reason many state governments across the United States have either raised the driving age or severely curtailed the initial freedoms a driver's license offers.)

Length of Midadolescence

Because today adolescence lasts up to fifteen years, a midadolescent has a more difficult time than did previous high-school-aged students seeing college and career as the hope of a secure and fulfilling future. Instead of looking forward to adulthood, the students I talked to said, "What's in it for me?" rather than "How am I going to make a difference in the world?"

Appeals to think about the future may motivate some midadolescents, but for the vast majority these appeals can easily become
one more adult mantra and therefore easily dismissed.

Lack of Ability in Abstract Thinking

It has generally been assumed that high-school-aged students
have the capacity for abstract thinking. During this study, however, I
observed that midadolescents' ability to engage in abstract thought
is limited to the immediate context of a discussion. I observed a
nearly universal inability to integrate the many layers of their lives
with any sense of abstract cohesion.

The most significant difference between midadolescents and late
adolescents is that late adolescents can cogently discuss multifaceted concepts that cut across social and relational lines in a way
that allows for the implications of that discussion to intersect at
any level, with any relationship. Midadolescents, on the other hand,
are fully capable of penetrating and insightful dialogue regarding
a variety of topics and issues, but when it comes to applying the
conclusions reached during these discussions to a relationship or
social reality, especially in a different social context, they cannot
see the connection.

Let me give you an example I experienced. Students would tell
me of the love they had for a parent and what this should mean
in terms of how they treated their parent. Yet a short time later,
they would make arrangements with a friend to deceive that same
parent and do something that could cause the parent great pain
and heartache. When I pointed out this incompatibility to the
students, they almost always rationalized or defended their inconsistent actions.

From Understanding to Action

I spend a good deal of time in the academic realm where scholars
discuss the latest research. I also spend time with parents and other
adults, who share with me their concerns and questions about
kids. And now that I have been privileged to see the world from
the eyes of the kids themselves, I want to help adults do a better
job of caring for the kids in their lives.

29

This is not a how-to book but rather a wake-up call designed to challenge every adult to recognize and struggle with what our choices as adults have done to the children of our society.

As we will see in the next chapter, the major consequence of adult inattention has been a profound sense of abandonment among today's teens. And as I hope to show in the chapters that follow, the only solution to this problem is for adults to roll up our sleeves and invest ourselves in the lives of the individual young people we know.

2

abandoned and all alone

After graduating from college, Christopher McCandless wanted to get away—far away. So he gave his grad school savings to charity and left his family's comfortable East Coast home to go on a journey that took him across the continent to California.

But California was only another step for Chris, who had his heart set on Alaska. After gathering food and supplies, he headed out to the land beyond roads and trails where, after spending more than one hundred days alone in the rugged wilderness, he died from starvation. His emaciated body was found by hunters in an abandoned bus.

Chris's story is told in *Into the Wild*, John Krakauer's bestselling 1996 book that was turned into an acclaimed 2007 movie by writer/director Sean Penn.

From the surface it looks like Chris abandoned his family and "the world," but if you look deeper you can see that Chris saw things the other way around. As he saw it, his parents—who had deceived the family about their relationship and their previous divorces—had abandoned him, leaving him to make his own way in the world.

Part of what makes Chris's story resonate with readers and viewers is that all of us have felt abandoned at times. But as I learned

31

during my journey into the world of today's teens, abandonment is a normal and accepted part of their lives.

As you will see in this chapter and book, I argue that abandonment is the fundamental cultural reality of kids today. This makes perfect sense to some readers, but others aren't so sure. They see kids in large groups at school or at church events, and they say, "This doesn't look like abandonment to me."

But let's look more closely at the lives of kids and see if signs of systemic abandonment become clearer. And as we look more closely, may we be inspired by the words of my middle son, a high school junior, who gave me this warning when I started this journey: "I know you think you know a lot about kids, Dad, but you had better be ready for a shock. I don't think you really get it! I don't think any adult gets it!"

Better or Worse, Revisited

As we saw in chapter 1, experts disagree about whether contemporary youth face brave new challenges that kids have never faced before or whether today's kids are basically dealing with the same

Talking the Talk

Teens want their parents to talk with them about dating, sex, and the girl/guy next door. They just don't want them to talk too much. According to a survey by the National Campaign to Prevent Teen pregnancy, 88 percent of teens say it'd be easier to postpone having sex if they were able to talk to their parents more openly about such issues, and 59 percent say their parents are role models. But experts say that parents should be careful about how they go about such conversations. Typical parenting jargon ("Not while you're in MY house, you won't!") or even getting overly sappy often shuts down the very conversations the teens need. Experts advise parents to try to be good listeners—and to not freak out over what their children say.

kinds of problems kids have always dealt with. This disagreement carries over into our discussion of abandonment.

Pulitzer Prize–winning author Ron Powers made his perspective clear with the title of his controversial 2002 article in *Atlantic* magazine, "The Apocalypse of Adolescence." Powers also discussed the article on TV's *60 Minutes II*.

Powers argued that "the inconvenience of children, the downright menace of children—has become a dominant theme of life" for many adults. And his article explored a culture of disenfranchisement that is increasingly troubling many kids, resulting in violence and other ills.

On the other side of the debate is University of California, Santa Cruz, sociologist Mike Males, who says adolescents are in far better shape today than they have been in years. Today's young "are doing better than ever," he says in his 2002 *Los Angeles Times* article, "The New Demons: Ordinary Teens." Males says our fears about troubled teens are misplaced and overstated, leading to a dangerous condition he calls "Ephebiphobia" or "extreme fear of youth," an ailment that is propelled by a "full-blown media panic."

The debate continues. And while some people may wonder how two smart people could come to such opposed opinions, I look for the ways in which their views connect and overlap with each other. After listening to the debate by these and other experts, here's my conclusion: as adolescents attempt to navigate the increasing complexity of life, they are both incredibly resilient and deeply wounded.

Tufts University sociologist David Elkind explains it this way:

> [I]dentity formation requires a kind of envelope of adult standards, values and beliefs that the adolescent can confront and challenge in order to construct and test out her own standards, values and beliefs. . . . Today, however, adults have fewer standards, values and beliefs and hold on to them less firmly than was true in the past. The adolescent must therefore struggle to find an identity without the benefit of this supportive adult envelope.

On the surface, the adolescent world may appear to be relatively stable and healthy. Yet beneath the calm waters presented by positive empirical data, there is turmoil that is difficult, painful, lonely, and even harmful to our young. To become adults, adolescents need adults, but when adults are not present and involved in their lives, they are forced to figure out how to survive life on their own. Or as Patricia Hersch notes in *A Tribe Apart: A Journey into the Heart of American Adolescents*: "The more we leave kids alone, don't engage, the more they circle around on the same adolescent logic that has caused dangerous situations to escalate."

Today's teens may appear happy and secure from a distance, but the way midadolescents have been forced to design their own world and separate social system has created perhaps the most serious and yet understudied social crisis of our time. We hear such statements so often that it is easy to turn a skeptical or even deaf ear, but my hope is that the evidence emerging from this study is far too strong for even the most entrenched to ignore.

Our Culture of Abandonment

Elkind wrote his bestselling book, *The Hurried Child,* in 1981. In revised versions that appeared in 1988 and 2001, he made it clear that things had changed for the worse:

> Many of the problems that I described in the preface to the second edition have only gotten worse. The concept of child competence, which drove much of the hurrying of childhood in previous decades, is very much alive today. Parents are under more pressure than ever to overschedule their children and have them engage in organized sports and other activities that may be age-inappropriate. Unhappily, the overtesting of children in public schools has become more extensive than it was even a decade ago. In some communities even kindergarteners are given standardized tests. Media pressures to turn children into consumers have also grown exponentially.

When Elkind talks about hurrying, he is seeing some of the same problems that I see when I talk about abandonment by parents, teachers, and other adults who should be there for adolescents. In his 1994 book *Ties That Stress: The New Family Imbalance*, Elkind says:

34

Like all those whose needs are not being met over the long term, postmodern children and adolescents are feeling victimized. They believe that they must suppress their own needs for security and protection to accommodate their parents' and the society's expectations that they be independent and autonomous. Like modern mothers, postmodern young people either turn their anger on themselves (for letting themselves be used) or at the world around them.

Elkind is not alone in describing this transition. In *A Generation Alone: Xers Making a Place in the World,* authors William Mahedy and Janet Bernardi write that many youth say, "We know that no one really needs us."

And Patricia Hersch concludes: "The adolescents of the nineties are more isolated and more unsupervised than any other generation."

The Effect of Competition and Labels

A century ago scholars first began talking about this period of life we call adolescence. At that time only 10 percent of the population attended high school. Today more than 90 percent do.

Originally America's public schools were designed and structured with a common goal: to nurture emerging adolescents by providing systems, structures, and activities to help them grow into adulthood by means of the smoothest, most productive transition possible. And while these and other nurturing structures and movements were beneficial in many ways, a subtle change soon took place. These structures eventually distanced adults from the specific needs of adolescents.

By the time adolescents enter high school, nearly every one has been subjected to a decade or more of adult-driven and adult-controlled programs, systems, and institutions that are primarily concerned with adults' agendas, needs, and dreams. Here are some examples of how far we have drifted from a personal commitment to the young:

- Families with eight- and nine-year-old boys pay hundreds if not thousands of dollars to spend Thanksgiving weekend traveling so their boys can "have the opportunity of a lifetime"

35

to play in a contrived, skillfully marketed, mythical peewee football "national championship."

- An eight-year-old who loves to dance is no longer allowed to attend a class she loves for its fun, free, raucous, hour-and-a-half adventure in tights. Her dancing now consists of up to six (or more) hours of training, repetition, and practice per week, culminating in something called a "dance competition," a phrase that was formerly an artistic oxymoron.

- Parental fistfights erupt during a seven-year-olds' T-ball game in what I was later told is "an intense competitive atmosphere" because it is, "after all, competitive T-ball!"

- A high school junior arrives home from school promptly at 5:30 after volleyball practice and begins a four- to six-hour ordeal called homework—on an average night. She has dinner over a textbook, which allows her to avoid conversation with her mom, and falls asleep exhausted at midnight, only to rise the next morning at 5:30 for band practice before her 7:00 AP calculus class.

What is interesting is that many adults will highlight these and other activities as proof of their commitment to the young. "I drive my kid to all of these activities. I sacrifice my life, work, avocation, and enjoyment to take the kids to soccer games, concerts, and competitions."

Ironically this statement reveals the subtle spread of abandonment. We have evolved to the point where we believe driving is support, being active is love, and providing any and every opportunity is selfless nurture. We are a culture that has forgotten how to be together. We have lost the ability to spend unstructured downtime. Rather than being with children in creative activities at home or setting them free to enjoy semi-supervised activities, such as "play," we as a culture have looked to outside organizations and structured agendas to fill their time and dictate their lives.

The problem is not simply the organized activities or sports. It is the cumulative effect that children experience as they grow up in today's social structure. Sports, music, dance, drama, Scouts, and even faith-related programs are all guilty of ignoring the de-

What, Me Worry?

Teens say that alcohol and drug use among their friends is pretty common. Parents say it's pretty rare. And therein lies a big problem, according to experts.

A recent study showed that 27 percent of teens ranked alcohol as their biggest concern, and that 50 percent had attended a party where drugs or alcohol had been used. In contrast, only 12 percent of parents felt that drugs or alcohol were concerns for their children, and 80 percent thought the parties their kids attended were alcohol- and drug-free.

velopmental needs of each individual young person in favor of the organization's goals.

Add to this the increasing amount of homework being assigned to students at younger and younger ages. The systemic pressure on American children is immense.

Too many of us actually enjoy the athletic, cultural, or artistic babysitting service that the paid staff or volunteers of an organization provide. Even with the best of intentions, the way we raise, train, and even parent our children today exhibits attitudes and behaviors that are simply subtle forms of parental abandonment.

This cultural shift has changed our priorities. The good of the unique individual has now been supplanted by a commitment to the good of the larger community, whether it is the team, school, club, class, or organization. Even very young children learn that they are only as valuable as their ability to contribute. By the time these students reach middle adolescence, they show signs of the rejection they have been subjected to throughout their lives.

As one community leader of youth sports told me, "They have to learn this lesson sometime—that they either are or aren't an athlete. It is better to find out when they are young." I wondered, *Better for whom?*

All this heightened competition requires young people to place tremendous emphasis on self-protection and self-promotion, making it increasingly difficult for even the best teacher, coach, or youth

How We Subtly Abandon Our Kids

Mark Cannister

As I was discussing this issue with a group of youth workers, focusing on how we abandon students in our churches and ministries, I realized quickly it's usually not as obvious as when a youth leader leaves the church and the students feel abandoned. Rather, we typically abandon students in very subtle ways. We abandon them when we declare that they're not old enough to be an usher or not mature enough to help collect the offering or they would be too much of a distraction to pass around the communion trays or read Scripture or sing in the "adult" choir or play in the "adult" worship band.

I also realized that we abandon students when we build relationships with them; then they don't *do* what we want (commit to Christ, participate in a Bible study, go to camp, and so on), so we move on to other kids who *will* do what we want, leaving the first ones in our wake. Even in the midst of building relationships with the best of intentions, we may be talking with one student when another student arrives. Without so much as an "excuse me," we abandon the conversation as though the first student disappeared right in the middle of a sentence, and we engage the student we haven't seen in a few weeks or the student who's scheduled to lead worship that night or the student who won the big game Friday night.

I've realized that relational abandonment also happens when students move from the middle school ministry to the high school ministry while the middle school volunteers stay behind—modeling *conditional* love. Adults sacrifice long-term relationships with kids (I care about this kid and will work with him/her over the long haul) to the bureaucratic regimes of accepted youth ministry practice (I am a middle school vol-

worker to "waste" the time it takes to walk alongside an individual adolescent, much less create an environment in which each one is uniquely nurtured and led.

A child who seems relatively slow, distracted, insecure, or otherwise handicapped (according to the dictates of the organization) has little chance of being considered anything other than one needy but incompetent face among many.

One day when I was working with a teacher in preparation for substituting in her class, she illustrated this attitude perfectly, if unintentionally. "My morning class has three or four great kids," she said, "but the afternoon class is full of average kids, and are they ever

unteer, *not* a high school volunteer). Our care is based on a student's age. In essence, we communicate: "As long as you're in middle school, I'll love you, but now that you're in high school, our relationship is over." We do the same thing when students go off to college. It would seem that we have a long way to go in understanding genuine unconditional love. How subtly we abandon students without even realizing it, yet they feel the pain all the same!

Abandonment has also become a strong theme in my seminars for parents of teenagers. While the fallout from divorce is a classic example of parental abandonment, the more subtle instances of abandonment are just as important to recognize and combat. Too often we create "reward" systems in our families to encourage children to do better in school or in sports or at church and we unintentionally communicate that our love is based on their performance. Likewise, our child is so excited to share a story with us or ask us a question, but often our only response is "Not now"; "I'm too tired"; "Can we talk about it later?" as if our teenager will be ready to talk anytime, anyplace. We know better than that.

As parents we abandon our kids when we leave their faith formation to others. Youth leaders and children's ministers will provide wonderful influences for our kids, but ultimately it is our responsibility to nurture the faith of our children. While there is truth in the familiar saying, "It takes a village to raise a child," too often we parents abandon our children to the village and use the cliché to abdicate our responsibility. We need to be thankful for the responsibility and privilege we have been given and sacrificially engage in the lives of our children.

Our church recently faced the daunting obligation of performing a funeral service for a teenager who was killed in a car accident. Hundreds of teenagers and adults filled the sanctuary for a moving service. But after the service a picture of abandonment

a pain." This comment disturbed me deeply. She had been a teacher for only five or six years, but she had already learned automatically to divide all her students into two groups: great and average.

Today many young people feel the effects of such judgments. Some children and adolescents rise to the top early through a unique skill, a quick wit or tongue, or an attractive look, style, or quality. Others learn how to cope with recurring abandonment by adopting a countercultural style or persona. Many kids discover at a very young age that adults judge them to be either an achiever or a challenge, and they go through life feeling the weight of these judgments.

emerged. Clusters of kids in tears filled the church lobby, while nearly all the adults gathered in the fellowship hall. Few adults, beyond the youth leaders, were helping students grieve, and we can't assume that students know how to handle such circumstances on their own.

So I find myself working hard these days with youth workers and parents to expose the abandonment that teenagers are experiencing. Once the abandonment is exposed, the solutions are often rather simple—let students serve and lead, stick with them long term, maintain relationships, make time for them, listen to their stories, empathize with their pain, engage their culture, and embrace our responsibility.

As parents and youth leaders, we need to recognize the abandonment in our culture and our ministries, get our hands dirty, and commit ourselves to the students God has entrusted to our care, working to undo this scourge of abandonment. We must learn to become the voice of deliberate kindness, careful nurturance, and dedicated compassion.

> Love the LORD your God with all your heart and with all your soul and with all your strength. These commandments that I give you today are to be upon your hearts. Impress them on your *children*. Talk about them when you sit at home and when you walk along the road, when you lie down and when you get up.
>
> Deuteronomy 6:5–7

Mark Cannister serves as Professor of Youth Ministries at Gordon College in Wenham, Massachusetts, near Boston and has been involved in every aspect of youth ministry over the last thirty years.

Members of both groups, the achievers and the challenges, are known as such by teachers and the administration and are therefore given the greatest amount of energy and attention. But there is a third category, and it is the largest group of all: the middle or average student, who has not, for a variety of reasons, taken the steps necessary to be labeled an achiever or a challenge. Most of the time these middle students go through life without being noticed or appreciated by adults. Even though they make up about 80 percent of the teen population, typically these middle kids get only 20 percent of adults' attention, while the 20 percent of teens who are achievers or challenges get 80 percent of adults' attention.

During my journey, I sought to understand kids in all three of these groups. When I got to know some of the achiever kids who were noticed, I realized they clearly *knew* they were noticed because of something they produced, displayed, or created. These kids wore their uniqueness—intelligence, athleticism, wittiness, respectability—like a cloak. But underneath the surface, even the top achievers shared a great fear of being found out and losing everything they had worked so hard to attain. "I have to get the grades and play sports," confided one senior male student who carried a 4.0 grade point average, started in a major sport, and seemed well liked and respected by everyone on campus. "I have nothing else."

This student's comment illustrates how even those students who are seen as having it all perceive themselves to have much less than that. If a top achiever feels this way, imagine the feelings of abandonment experienced by the majority of kids who don't get such affirmation and support.

Abandonment in Interpersonal Relationships

Systemic abandonment is what happens when the adults and institutions that should have a nurturing role in the lives of young people ignore or turn against them. There is also a "felt" dimension: that nobody really cares about me. This "felt" part may be something that all kids in all ages have felt, rightly or wrongly, but today the abandonment is real and systemic.

The experience of systemic abandonment is not confined to schools and other places where kids gather in large numbers. Adolescents have also suffered the loss of safe relationships and intimate settings that once served as the primary sources of nurture and community for those traveling the path to adulthood.

The most obvious example of this is in the family. Members of the postmodern family are often so concerned about the needs, struggles, and issues of parents that the emotional and developmental needs of the children go largely unaddressed. When combined with the disappearance of stable, extended families, the de-emphasizing of the importance of marriage, and the lack of healthy relationships with adults as friends and mentors, it is easy to see why today's adolescents face an internal crisis of unprecedented scope.

The loss of meaningful relationships with adults has been the most powerful force in adolescents' systemic abandonment.

41

Learning to Just Be

Drew Sams

For years we had tried to make students "busy for Jesus" by providing exciting events and programs that they would want to do. The success of our ministry had always been measured by the number of students attending, and if a student came to all of our events, we assumed he or she was spiritually healthy. Wow, were we wrong!

It all came to a grinding halt when one of our "all-star" students attempted to commit suicide. While we had arbitrarily labeled him a successful student in our ministry because he attended every weekend service, was in a small group, served on mission trips, and was an active part of our leadership team, we had essentially "abandoned" him to the point that we didn't even know he had been dating his girlfriend for over six months, was struggling with purity, and was seriously doubting his faith.

When we began to see teenagers in our community through "abandonment-colored glasses," our eyes were opened. We realized we had been unknowingly contributing to the vicious cycle of abandonment—and we were the church!

We have now become a community that is remembering again what it means just to be together. One of the many practical ways we have done this is through equipping volunteers, parents, and students to *be present* in each other's lives. Our events calendar is emptier than it used to be, but now we are free to go to students, listen, and care unconditionally for them by truly being the church.

Drew Sams is currently serving as Pastor of Student Ministries at Calvary Community Church in Westlake Village, California, and is one of the contributing authors to a collaborative youth ministry blog at www. collectionofcrumbs.com.

Because midadolescents have not had enough life experience to understand fully the accompanying sense of loneliness and isolation they feel, few of the ones I talked with verbalized their experience as "loss," but the feeling of loss oozed out of nearly every student. When the kids I got to know felt safe enough to admit it, each student I talked to acknowledged that loneliness is a central experience of his or her life.

One expert compared the experience of today's teens to a group of kids swimming in the sea. From a distance they may seem to be having the time of their lives, but on closer inspection it's clear they are not waving; they are drowning.

Counting the Cost of Abandonment

Like the cumulative effects of toxic chemicals in our water, the cumulative effects of abandonment are toxic. Children who experience abandonment struggle with the pain and fear associated with having no grounding or stability in their lives. Plus, their conflicts with parents or other adults short-circuit their ability to address their own needs in healthy ways.

Research has consistently shown that parental conflict forces children to sacrifice their own developmental needs to meet the needs of their parents—needs they are ill-equipped to meet. In fact they are often pushed into taking mediating roles when things get tough. Even young children are forced to take sides in parental conflict or to offer advice to a struggling parent.

Time spent with significant adults, especially parents, provides the most important environment for healthy adolescent development, but Patricia Hersch reports such times are rare:

> "In all societies since the beginning of time, adolescents have learned to become adults by observing, imitating and interacting with grown-ups around them," write Mihaly Csikzentmihalyi and Reed Larson in *Being Adolescent.* "It is therefore startling how little time [modern] teenagers spend in the company of adults." In their study Csikzentmihalyi and Larson found that adolescents spent only 4.8 percent of their time with their parents and only 2 percent with adults who were not their parents.

There are at least two major consequences of parental and adult abandonment:

- The adolescent journey is lengthened, because no one is available to help move the developmental process along.
- Adolescents know that they are essentially on their own, for as William Mahedy and Janet Bernardi argue, "aloneness is the enduring result of abandonment."

But adults can fight abandonment if they're willing to get involved in kids' lives.

Surprise! Adolescents Want Adults in Their Lives

Teens may not let adults know they need more of their time, but when I talk to them, this is what I hear. In facilitating a parent/youth event for a community group in Seattle, I asked students to compile a list of what they wanted adults to know about them. Many said they wanted more one-on-one time with the significant adults in their lives.

"We spend no time with adults from junior high on," said one student. "Maybe fifteen minutes every other day is the best we ever get."

Contrary to what most adults may think, middle adolescents want significant relationships with adults who care about them but they don't know how to pursue such relationships. And many teens feel adults are not trustworthy. For most of their lives they have experienced a lack of authentic concern from adults.

Systemic abandonment has created an environment in which midadolescents believe they are truly on their own. As a result, they go underground; they pull away from the adult world. This causes a uniquely ordered society, a world beneath, a world in which rules, expectations, a value system, and even social norms are created to maintain an environment in which the midadolescent can achieve the single most important goal of this stage of life: survival.

When I got close enough to young people by entering into their world and building trust with them, they let me look into their lives and their feelings of abandonment. And it was not just one or two voices crying out for connection. I heard an overwhelming chorus of longing to be cared for and to be taken seriously.

The social world of teens may appear impenetrable, but beyond the perceived hostility that surrounds the midadolescent is a fragile soul hidden behind a sophisticated layer of defense and protection. Even the most "solid" students confessed that life is far darker, far more violent, far more difficult, and far more tiring than adults, including their parents, realize.

Getting a Clue

"They have no clue, Dr. Clark." This assessment of adults' grasp of teen culture came from one of the top achievers I met during my journey. She maintained a 4.0 grade point average, was an

44

Going Where They Are

April Diaz

In our ministry to midadolescents, I realized we had contributed to systemic abandonment. For years I have asked adolescents to "come" to our events, run the ministry, and win their campuses for Christ. We have virtually eliminated the role of parents out of our own insecurity and fear. Maybe asking kids to come but having parents stay away are the two primary reasons that as many as 50 percent of adolescents leave faith in Jesus after high school.

This realization has changed *everything* for us: our vision, strategy, staffing, expectations, and mostly our hearts toward adolescents. I recognized, too, that my relationships with high school students were "rooted in my terms and created on *my* turf." We embraced the reality that if a student truly spends 99 percent of his or her life outside of the church, maybe our role in the church was to move toward students in their two greatest spaces: school (75 percent) and home (24 percent).

We have changed our vision to become a church without walls. Everything we engage in is intensely driven around holistic adolescent ministry—caring about the whole student's life—which includes going to their campus, where they spend most of their time; and partnering with parents, the number one influence in their lives. We're no longer primarily concerned about their attendance in our weekly programs but about how they will one day be integrated into the larger global community.

We agree that if the church has a hope in reaching the next generation, we have to become like water and flow into adolescents' culture, just like Jesus did for us.

April Diaz is Next Gen Pastor at NewSong Church in Irvine, California, where she has been for four years. Secretly, she's a total girlie girl, reads more than she can put into practice, and still drools over her husband of more than seven years.

all-league volleyball player, and was one of the more respected students on campus.

"But you seem like you are managing it all pretty well," I responded.

"Yeah," she said, "I'm pretty good at it, huh?"

What she meant was, "I'm good at playing the game, maintaining the show, and somehow surviving the obstacles. But inside things aren't as nice as they seem."

At the risk of sounding depressing, my journey revealed to me that many young people are one step away from the abyss of isolation and despair. One articulate junior reminded me of this with the words of a poem:

> You come into the world alone.
> You go out into the world alone.
> In life you have no friends.

These heartfelt lines serve as an indictment of the culture of abandonment that adults have bequeathed to today's teens. And the only way to turn things around is to undo this systemic abandonment and enter with care and compassion into the world of the young people we know. As we enter their world, we must be determined to listen, to see, and ultimately to understand the destructive circumstances that adult abandonment has helped foster.

By the time our children reach high school and middle adolescence, they are aware that for most of their lives they have been pushed, prodded, and molded to become people whose value rests in their ability to serve someone else's agenda. Whether it is a coach, a schoolteacher, a parent, a music teacher, or a Sunday school counselor, midadolescents believe intuitively that nearly every adult they have encountered has been subtly (or not so subtly) out to get something from them. When this awareness begins to take root during middle adolescence, it leads to frustration, anger, and a sense of betrayal. These feelings drive the experience of abandonment that defines contemporary midadolescence.

Many adults are too wrapped up in their own problems to see or care about the problems their children are facing. They are like the laid-back commune dwellers in T. C. Boyle's *Drop City*, his bestselling novel about the 1960s: "They didn't want to save children, they wanted to *be* children." Other adults are too attached to their own memories of the "good old days" of their youth to realize that today's kids are coming of age in a far more complex and challenging world.

Meanwhile, most midadolescents address their abandonment instinctively by attempting to find a safe place from which to live out one of the most difficult and challenging developmental periods they will ever face.

It is my hope that you and the many other men and women reading this book will be agents of change who turn the tide away from systemic abandonment to intentional engagement in the life of today's teens. If you're interested in this challenging but rewarding assignment, read on as we explore the complex inner and outer lives of today's teens.

3

exploring the world beneath

Chuck Noland was a hardworking, time-obsessed FedEx executive who hoped to marry his fiancée as soon as he could tame his globetrotting travel schedule. Then on one international flight everything changed.

The cargo jet on which Chuck was a passenger crashed into the ocean, and Chuck washed up on a deserted island. While struggling for survival and dreaming of sailing back to civilization, he created civilization of a kind in the cave where he slept.

If you've ever seen Tom Hanks in the movie *Cast Away*, you'll recognize this summary. But what's interesting to me is to see how today's teens are just as obsessed with survival in their world as Chuck Noland was on his island. And some teens even seek security in underground caves.

By entering their worlds (and their caves, if they invite us), we can begin to understand a major phenomenon of teen life I call "the world beneath." Let me explain.

Going Underground

Within the first few weeks of stepping out on my adventure into the world of today's teens, I came to two conclusions. First, the vast majority of adults simply do not comprehend the complex and varied worlds in which nearly all midadolescents dwell. Second, most adults fear and in many cases are basically repulsed by what they see in the adolescent world.

As Patricia Hersch wrote in *A Tribe Apart*: "Adolescents today inhabit a world largely unknown to adults." And opinion polls that have asked adults their feelings about teens have found that the words "rude" and "wild" are commonly used to describe them.

It is really very simple to understand what has happened, at least in concept. Kids feel abandoned by the adults in their lives and rejected by much of the world around them, so they have responded by creating their own worlds where they feel safe and secure. Midadolescents have responded to systemic abandonment by creating their own separate and highly structured social systems. These social webs constitute what I call the world beneath.

There have always been social differences between youth and adults, but what I have been seeing is different from the concepts of "youth culture" or "generation gap" that have been tossed around for decades.

The world beneath has been evolving over several decades, but in recent years it has undergone a shift: from a rather innocuous and at times innocent withdrawal to a more intentional and defensive separation from the "adult" world into a unique social system. The world beneath has its own rules of relating, moral code, and defensive strategies that are well-known to midadolescents and are tightly held secrets of their community.

Earlier in this book I discussed the impact of the '60s. Other observers have sought to blame these shifts in the world beneath on culprits like rock music, Hollywood movies, television, technology, or even the Industrial Revolution. And some adults have blamed adolescents for the way kids have rebelled against society and the values these adults hold dear. But I maintain that the primary force at work in this shift is adults, who have—by their neglect—pushed adolescents away and forced them to create their own subterranean subculture.

50

Castaways Seeking a Safe Harbor

There are three major ways that the systemic abandonment we described in the previous chapter has shaped kids' social worlds:

1. Adolescents intuitively believe they have no choice but to create their own world. To survive, they have to band together and burrow beneath the surface to create their own safe place.
2. Because midadolescents sense an emotional and relational starvation, the most important thing in their lives is a relationally focused home where they know they are welcome.
3. Midadolescents have an amazing ability to band together in a way that satisfies their longing to connect while helping

Youth Culture Update

Privacy? What's That?

Forget what Grandma told you about children being "seen, not heard." Thanks to the Internet, today's teens expect to be seen and heard by their friends, acquaintances—even perfect strangers. And they're A-OK with that.

According to experts, youth have a completely different understanding of the word "privacy," thanks to living in an age loaded with reality television, cell phone cameras, and, of course, the World Wide Web. Social networking sites like MySpace and Facebook have changed the way teens interact with one another, and today's youth may regularly converse with dozens of "friends" at a time via instant messaging.

"The private self and public self become intertwined in a way that we can't possibly understand," said psychologist Linda Young, who writes about teens and technology. "So they're not embarrassed about some of the things that we think they should be embarrassed about because it's an extension of the self that they're used to having viewed."

them navigate the conflicting and at times harrowing journey of adolescence.

Like the farmer in *Field of Dreams* who felt he had no choice but to build the baseball field at the bidding of a persistent yet elusive voice, every adolescent hears an equally compelling internal voice calling him or her to build the world and social setting he or she so desperately wants. Rejected by the adult world, teens have gone in search of greatly needed "social capital," whether it is vital relationships, moral and ethical guidelines, or other factors that will help them figure out who they are and where they fit in. Or as Robert Putnam put it in his book *Bowling Alone*:

> The absence of positive norms, community associations, and informal adult friendship and kin networks leaves kids to their own devices. It is in such settings that youths are most likely to act on shortsighted or self-destructive impulses. It is in such settings too that youths are most prone to create their own social capital in the form of gangs or neighborhood "crews."

Anne Rice explored similar issues through a character in her novel, *Belinda*:

> I had my first period when I was nine. . . . I was wearing a C-cup bra by the time I was thirteen. The first boy I ever slept with was shaving every day at fifteen; we could have made babies together. . . . But what is a kid here? . . . You can't legally smoke, drink, start a career, get married . . . all this for years and years after you're a physical adult. All you can do is play 'til you're twenty-one. . . . We're all criminals. . . . To be an American kid, you have to be a bad person. . . . Everybody's an outcast. Everybody's a faker.

Today's teens are both abandoned and resilient, and they desperately try to create places of safety and belonging, even as they say that they can take care of themselves and that they do not need anybody. As one teacher remarked, "I don't know why I keep hitting my head against the wall. Maybe the kids are right when they tell me that I don't know them or understand them and that they are fine without me. Sometimes I just don't know anymore why I even bother." Many adults have felt confusion or frustration when their

Feminine Side of Cyberspace

Teen girls are far more likely to be heavily involved in online networking than boys, according to a recent study from the Pew Internet and American Life Project. According to Pew, 35 percent of girls ages twelve to seventeen have created a blog, compared with just 20 percent of boys. They're more likely to belong to a social network site, such as MySpace or Facebook, and they're more likely to post pictures too.

The study also found that teens from poorer, less educated households are more likely to blog, and that hardly anyone under age eighteen regularly emails these days.

"Email is not the primary way you talk to your friends," said Amanda Lenhard, one of the report's authors. "It's used to talk with groups, if you're planning something complicated and you need to send long, letterlike messages."

efforts to reach out to young people appeared to be rejected. That's natural. But don't forget this important truth: every midadolescent is crying out for an adult who cares.

Have you ever seen the History Channel program called *Cities of the Underworld*? In every episode host Don Wildman explores the hidden history and mysteries found underneath the cities and streets of the world. We need to adopt a similar approach as we tunnel beneath the observable adult landscape in search of the world that today's teens have created for their own relational safety and security.

Every person wants to fit in with others and to find his or her sense of place in the world. The world beneath allows teens to find the safety they need, and this security allows them to address the varied tasks they must handle in contemporary culture, including:

- determining how to navigate the multiple expectations of teachers, parents, and other adults while maintaining satisfying and fulfilling adolescent relationships

Acknowledging the Very Real Emotions of Teens

Kelly Soifer

Having worked with youth for more than twenty-five years, I am more convinced than ever that kids desire unconditional relationships with adults.

All other adults in a student's life "have to" love them—parents, teachers, and coaches are expected to relate to them and seem to demand particular results from them all the time. Yet youth workers—especially volunteer leaders—*choose* to enter a relationship with students. And if these adults pursue these friendships diligently, relying on Christ's love rather than their own limited affections, students are easily won over.

This became especially evident to me recently in walking with our young people as three horrific deaths pierced the armor of youthful invincibility that most teenagers have. People this young aren't "supposed to" die! Our students felt vulnerable and afraid. Worse still, these painful losses made many of them feel abandoned by the One who supposedly will never leave them—God himself. "If he's so loving, how could he allow our friends to die?"

Teens' emotions are raw and elemental, and their thoughts morph daily. We had to be committed to riding that roller coaster with them. This journey was all the more poignant for me in that I was dealing with my own grief. A longtime friend and former volunteer died of cancer in the midst of this season. As I saw others struggle, often awkwardly, to care for me and for others closest to the ordeal, I was reminded of what works (and certainly what doesn't!) in caring for those who grieve. Many believers go

- balancing loyalty to family with time for peers
- pleasing parents, coaches, teachers, and other adults while dealing with the pervasive sense of abandonment some adults create

Layer on Layer of Personas

It is also helpful to think of adolescents' social lives as made of layers of relationships, or even a variety of roles or personas that they adopt. The challenges listed above are but a sampling of the multiple layers of life within which every midadolescent must live. Each of these layers presents its own unique challenges, and therefore the cumulative effect is that midadolescents have the sense

to the book of Job when they face loss, depression, and tragedy. Often Job's "friends" and counselors are criticized, but they actually got it right when they "sat on the ground with him for seven days and seven nights. *No one said a word to him*, because they saw how great his suffering was" (Job 2:13).

I have counseled our volunteers not to be overly concerned by students' anger, confusion, and doubt. God seems to be able to handle all of these reactions and more, as we see when we read through the book of Psalms! In this season, students felt abandoned by the schools, by adults, and by each other, as they discovered that their grief didn't seem to end, yet the conversations about their losses did. Together we recognize that God has not abandoned us!

Chap Clark's book *Hurt* asserts that "the loss of safe relationships and intimate settings that [serve] as the primary nurturing community for those traveling the path from child to adult" is a major form of abandonment experienced by today's youth. I couldn't agree more. In our post–9/11 world, students feel valued only if they have a résumé full of activities and accomplishments that will somehow ensure "success" in a frightening and overwhelming world. Instead, we need to show them that we take them seriously even without examining their résumés. They have very real emotions and thoughts. We cannot call them to productivity as much as to depth and authenticity.

Kelly Soifer is Pastor to Youth and Families (fifth through twelfth grades) at Santa Barbara Community Church, where she has been on staff since 1994. Previous to that, she worked in a variety of capacities with Young Life on the Central Coast.

of a highly volatile, at times hostile, world. The world beneath provides midadolescents the respite they need to survive the aggressive anonymity of the high school world.

Today's midadolescents have been forced to live according to the layers of personas that define them. As Susan Harter and her colleagues report in their study, "The Complexity of the Self in Adolescence":

> [Adolescents develop a] proliferation of selves that vary as a function of the social context. These include self with father, mother, close friend, romantic partner, peers, as well as the self in the role of student, on the job, and as athlete. . . . A critical developmental task of adolescence, therefore, is the construction of multiple selves in different roles and relationships.

The more I observed today's teens, the more convinced I became that the young people who will emerge from adolescence in best shape are those who seem able to switch roles and personas as rapidly as a play actor switches costumes. I listened as a sophomore girl, who described herself as active in church, convinced me that she loved her parents more than anyone else and that she would never do anything to hurt them. Yet almost immediately afterward she engaged in a profanity-laced conversation with a friend as she described her sexual relationship with a boy she had met the previous weekend. Clearly I was within earshot of this discussion, yet she seemed oblivious to my presence. When she turned back to me a few minutes later, I admitted to her that I had overheard a bit of her conversation.

"How would your parents feel if they had heard you?" I asked her.

She simply smiled. "What they don't know won't hurt them."

"Would you lie to your parents if they guessed anything?"

"Of course. Well, not lie, exactly, but I know that they would be mad at me, and so I would make sure that they would not find out the truth."

This winsome, attractive, and deceptive young woman did not see the contradiction between her behavior and her attitude. She lived her life in multiple layers and did not bother to seek out connections or contradictions between her relationships with her parents (the adult world) and her friends (the world beneath).

Most young people have learned to become adept at changing roles whenever it is needed. Of course the home base of midadolescents is the world beneath. That is where they feel safest and most secure. When they surface to enter the adult world, they view this as a temporary excursion into potentially hostile territory that is essentially unsafe.

Adults who work with kids in school, church, sports, or other settings need to realize that most teens view the layers of life that adults order and control (or even those under the influence of an adult-controlled system, such as a student-led and -run endeavor like the school yearbook, student council, and so on) as alien territory. The personas they adopt in these settings are much different from the roles they play in the world beneath.

Also adults need to see that kids have become adept at making adults believe that the selves they see are the entire package. But when we come into contact with kids in an adult arena, we are seeing only the tip of the iceberg. Most of their reality lies hidden beneath the surface.

This was an incredibly discouraging revelation as I reflected on my own years of work with midadolescents. The person I cared for, taught, counseled, and even befriended was not the true, authentic, unfiltered self that friends saw. What parent of a contemporary midadolescent has not heard the complaint: "You don't even know me. The only people who know me are my friends!" For midadolescents, this is not an idle gripe. It is the reality of their multilayered lives.

And as I got to know more and more students, I found this multilayered, multiple-persona approach to be true of white students as well as Asian, Latino, African American, and even Eastern European teens. It's easy for many young people to look beyond barriers caused by nationality, race, or ethnicity. But asking them to live without their layers would cause internal and external meltdown. They simply could not cope without their carefully crafted world.

Studies have shown that while ethnic adolescents tend to reject their parents' rules and norms, just as those in the dominant culture do, they do not reject identification with their ethnicity. In the world beneath, all students are looking for a safe place, even when in that world there remain ethnic and socioeconomic subgroups.

In short, my experiences and research show that most midadolescents are basically healthy and solid young people who are desperately trying to make sense of a life made almost unbearably difficult by adult society.

There are several wonderful things to be said about the state of contemporary adolescence. I was amazed by the young people I got to know and was impressed by their creativity, resilience, inner strength, and determination. At the same time, I could not escape the feeling that many of today's teens are like the vaudevillian entertainer who spins plates atop slender poles. The most successful students seem to be those who are most

Finding Our Way into Closed Teen Groups

Jamie Eitel

A new church had started a drop-in ministry near a high school, where students could come on their breaks to eat pizza and play basketball. But only some of the students who came participated in the activities. Others retreated and sat along a wall of the gym until the break time was over.

This was a living example of what Chap Clark has identified as "the world beneath." These students were operating at such a high level of abandonment that any new adult presence was immediately met with suspicion and distrust. My "coolness quotient" would never be high enough to walk into their gathering without being invited. Plus, our context of basketball presented them with the expectation of being told that they weren't good enough to play. I would need to wait until I was invited into their groups.

I decided to see what I could do to get more students involved. I organized a simple four-on-four tournament format, and purchased a scoreboard to let them know the time they had before class. The score was less about achieving and more about keeping a rotation to allow more teams to play. Over the next eight weeks, students who used to hang out along the walls of the gym began to engage with others who were there.

Over the next few months, there would be lunch hours when certain regulars weren't able to be at the games. Faced with the possibility of not having players to form a team, the regulars would ask spectators to join their team, regardless of skill level. As the lunch hour progressed, I watched as these new players were integrated by the regulars, allowing a genuine sense of play to be born underneath the guise of a normally competitive activity.

skilled at getting the greatest number of plates to spin at once. Bonus points are awarded if they can pull this off while making it look easy.

But both performer and audience know that the professional plate spinner is only one small misstep away from having the entire show fall to pieces. And many of today's teens have learned to live with the constant anxiety that no matter how fast they keep things spinning, their whole world may come crashing down around them at any minute. Meanwhile, the energy required to keep up the show is taking a tremendous toll on the hearts and psyches of midadolescents.

One day, when all the regulars were present, a group of these "substitutes" presented themselves as a team in the rotation. As they took to the floor, a voice from the wall called out, "Dream Team," half mockingly, half with anticipation of what might happen. As the game progressed, the regulars played with their usual intensity, but the cheers from the crowd had shifted from the regulars to those who were awkwardly tripping over themselves with each pass. Every move that contained some element of hope was met with cheers from the sidelines. Even the regulars began to give advice.

As the regulars inched toward a shutout victory, one of the Dream Team members was open and took the shot—it went in! Everyone exploded with cheers; the Dream Team was ecstatic (to the point of losing the game), but this was the beginning of their legacy. Soon Facebook wallposts appeared, talking about the first point scored in Dream Team history.

With that point, I saw a change in the attitude of the game—facing an adult world of abandonment, these adolescents rediscovered the joy of play that no longer included a performance-based evaluation of their character, but rather acceptance and encouragement.

Despite the limited vision of the leadership, I was able to recruit seven volunteers (average age of sixty-three) within the time span of two years, and watch God show these "grandparents" the hurt that lived deep in the lives of these teens and how their response of kindness and gentleness to these kids was a greater gospel than any preacher could ever present. The "Pizza Drop-In" had become their "church"—a place where they had met with God through interactions with his people.

Jamie Eitel is Pastor of Youth and Young Adults at Mississauga City Baptist Church near Toronto, Canada, and is also part of the adjunct faculty at Tyndale University College.

Mixed Messages

The most visible mark of the world beneath is the callousness that most adolescents wear like a defiant badge of honor when adults try to penetrate where they have not been invited. Often adults mistake this air of callousness for a genuine hardness and indifference, thus further perpetuating the distance between them and the teens in their life. And frankly, some adults find kids frightening and confusing, so when they feel kids are being indifferent or hard, some adults retreat. But my experience with kids revealed a different picture. Their apparent aloofness is not true hostility. It is self-protection born of abandonment, insecurity, and fear.

Midadolescents have little faith in adults and therefore do not trust them with the intimate reality of their lives. These fragile young people are not trying to be callous. Instead, they are wearing their toughness like a shield to protect themselves from further disappointment, and it's an exhausting and never-ending game. Midadolescents know that many adults really do care and are worthy of trust, but for most the risk of trusting is too great and yet they are so tired of keeping up the pretense.

One junior gave me a poem he had written to explore this uncertainty and unease.

Step into the Dark

Step into the dark where no one can see
Step into the dark where all you see is me
Step into the dark where there is suffering and pain
Step into the dark where not a single person knows your
    name
Step into the dark where the only color is black
Step into the dark where love is a mystery
Step into the dark where real men don't come back
Step into the dark where no one leaves tracks
Step into the dark where hell is a block away
Step into the dark where you might brighten my day

The world beneath exists because midadolescents believe that few if any adults genuinely care about them. Over a decade ago Hillary Clinton wrote an appeal for community involvement called *It Takes a Village*. But most of today's teens have no village they can call home in the adult world, so they create a safe place that feels like home.

What has caused this distance? You and I have. Adults have contributed to the worlds beneath by not swiftly and decisively putting a stop to any and all forms of abandonment. We have stood by and allowed a small group of teachers to belittle, authorities to ridicule, coaches to discourage, and parents to neglect and abuse. As Patricia Hersch puts it: "Aloneness makes adolescents a tribe apart."

Today's adolescents are indescribably lonely. They cling to their friends in the world beneath because they feel they have no other choice. As adolescence has lengthened and midadolescence has become more amorphous and its members more set apart, they have begun to wonder if anyone truly cares about them.

Sure, friends care, but only insofar as they are able to maintain the norms of their peer group. And many adults care, but they must show a great deal of love and make enormous effort to counteract what one destructive Sunday school teacher, Little League coach, or piano teacher said or did so long ago. Meanwhile, our kids keep their collective chin up and make the best of their world beneath.

A Tale of Two Worlds

Charles Dickens began his *Tale of Two Cities* with the famous line: "It was the best of times, it was the worst of times." I can say the same about the world today's teens inhabit.

As I spent time with young people, I had the privilege with certain students to sit on the steps of their secret world. I saw encouraging and positive things even in the crevices of that world. I saw genuine kindness and loyalty. I heard lofty dreams and honest stories. I saw flashes of light.

Yet as I sat on the steps of their world, I also witnessed palpable darkness. I heard vicious and vile conversations. I saw new levels of vulgarity that I found astonishing. I saw tremendous pain masked by obnoxious defiance, an insatiable selfishness, and indescribable cruelty. Even with all the good, the world beneath is filled with dark corners and hidden crevices.

We adults who care have a long way to go to penetrate the layers of protection that keep us from being one more disappointment in a world filled with them. But I am convinced that we are welcome in the lives of our teens if we are serious about going there and loving and caring when we are admitted to the sacred space of their souls.

Many of us have bought into the myth that our young people are doing fine. Some of us really believe it. For others among us,

61

this is just a convenient excuse from selfless involvement in the lives of kids who need us.

The two most important things we can do are:

- Try to understand the midadolescent world.
- Lovingly provide boundaries for the teens in our lives in a way that will keep them from making destructive choices as they are keeping the plates spinning and trying to navigate this difficult passage we call adolescence.

I like the way Mary Pipher puts it: "When teenagers temporarily lose their heads, which most do, they need an adult to help them recover."

Now, if you're ready to join me in the next phase of our adventure, meet me in part 2, where we will take a closer look at eight key aspects of kids' lives.

inside the lives of today's teens

4

from cliques to clusters

The Changing Shape of Teens' Social Lives

The overwhelming sense of abandonment many kids experience shows up in all areas of their lives, especially in the ways they connect to other kids, as I discovered when talking to a high school junior named Kyle.

In a sense Kyle was one of the fortunate ones. His parents were happily married and they actively showed their care and support for him by cheering at his football games and encouraging his growth in other areas. But the longer we talked, the more I could see his pain and struggles.

Like the majority of young males, Kyle has issues with his father, a card-carrying "man's man" who Kyle says is "more into my football than I am." Kyle loves and even likes his dad but he senses somewhere deep inside that, while his father loves him, at times he is more interested in Kyle's accomplishments than in who his son is as a person.

Kyle is not as scarred by a painful "father wound" as some other teens are, but he sees his dad as a relatively distant taskmaster who is fixated on having a "successful" son.

IM So Embarrassed

Teens don't necessarily prefer to instant message their friends over talking with them face-to-face. But when it comes to avoiding embarrassment, they start warming up their thumbs.

An Associated Press–AOL poll indicates that 43 percent of teens use IM to say things they'd rather not say in person. "If they freak out or something, you don't see it," said seventeen-year-old Cassy Hobert. "And if I freak out, they don't have to see it."

The poll also found that 22 percent of teens have used IMs to ask someone out, and 13 percent have broken up through IM. :(

Kyle feels real love for his mom, but then he dropped this bombshell in our conversation: "My parents don't know me. The only people who really know me are my friends."

In part 1 we saw how nearly every adult system, structure, organization, and institution has abandoned adolescents. The impact of this abandonment is seen in different ways as kids make the journey from early adolescence to midadolescence.

In early adolescence, children do not have the cognitive ability to articulate their own abandonment, though many of them sense it. Still, because they are closer to childhood than adulthood, they invest in the familial relationships that gave them safety as children. They feel pain, but often, because they can't identify where it comes from, they turn to their parents and families to ease that pain—even if the family is the source of their problems.

During midadolescence things change as kids begin exercising the ability to apply abstract thought to their world. At roughly fourteen or fifteen years of age, adolescents begin to reflect on how they have been treated for much of their life, and it slowly dawns on many of them that they may have been abandoned by those who should have "been there" for them.

When I encouraged adolescents to talk about past disappointments, to bring these feelings to the surface, and to examine past and present systems and institutions that impacted them, the emotions expressed ranged from disappointment or mild sarcasm to outright bitterness and hostility. As we will see in this chapter, their sense of abandonment plays a powerful role in how they organize their social lives.

Connecting through Clusters

Back in the good old days of the 1950s and well into the 1980s, much of the typical high school student's life was organized around cliques, those groups of students who established their place on the teen pecking order.

The website *In the 80s* summarizes the different cliques that can be seen in popular movies like 1985's *The Breakfast Club* and 1989's *Heathers*:

- The Popular Group
- The Jocks
- The Nerds
- Valley Girls
- Rappers
- Skaters
- Surfers
- Hackers
- Losers
- Outcasts

Since then, major changes have taken place across all segments of society, particularly the high school sociological landscape. Today high schools are populated by smaller groupings of friends, or clusters, which navigate as a unit the complex network of social interdependence with a loyalty similar to that of a family.

Canadian youth worker Donald Posterski described the emerging new social order of clusters back in 1985:

A friendship cluster is more than just a circle of relationships. It is heart and soul of being young today. It is a place to belong. There is no formal membership. You are either in or you are not. Being in means you share many things: interests, experiences, intimate thoughts, problems, and triumphs of the day. Being in means you tune in to the same music, wear each other's sweaters, and generally just enjoy each other.

Today clusters function as a kind of family, complete with a set of respected and controlled expectations, loyalties, and values. Sometimes the flag for a cluster is a similar interest, such as a style of music or an affinity for online gaming. But the thing that really gives a cluster its power is a common, almost tribalistic bond and unifying social narrative—a grand story that gives meaning and cohesiveness to the cluster and defines who's in and who's not. For example, smart kids (or athletic/religious/attractive) are the *good* kids, and it's those kids who belong in our group. Conversely, most of our school's social patterns are determined by "winners" (kids who have succeeded at something), but our group consists of "losers" (those who aren't as fast, as attractive, or as competitive as the winners). This bond is the hallmark of the social group that nearly all midadolescents will rely on throughout their high school life.

The inability during midadolescence to balance disappointment over specific events, people, or institutions by separating the good from the bad drives the intense need for a safe place. Midadolescents gather in like-minded groups to protect themselves. This is the main reason clusters have replaced cliques in today's adolescent social economy: teens believe they have no alternative.

Understanding How Clusters Work

One of the most clearly observable aspects of contemporary midadolescence is the structure of kids' social worlds and the operational expectations of their peer relationships. A social hierarchy structures these associations, both friendships and romantic relationships. Students also arrange their daily tasks according to this socializing structure. This determines what hallway to walk down between classes, where to see friends, and with whom to go

You Are What You Buy?

Some things in life are priceless, says the commercial. For self-esteem, there's Visa.

A new study indicates that, as a child's self-esteem declines, their desire for material possessions goes up. Researchers have tied trends in materialism to age: a strong desire for consumer goods begins as early as eight or nine, then drops off between the ages of sixteen and eighteen. Tellingly, many children in these tween and teen years are beset by self-esteem issues.

"The level of materialism in teens is directly driven by self-esteem," says professor Deborah Roedder John of the University of Minnesota. "When self-esteem drops as children enter adolescence, materialism peaks. Then by late adolescence, when self-esteem rebounds, their materialism drops."

to homecoming. The parameters of day-to-day experiences flow directly from the phenomenon labeled "clustering."

The phenomenon of clustering appears to be far different from anything I experienced growing up in the 1970s and early 1980s, but it's poorly understood by adults and inaccurately portrayed in the media. While scholars have studied peer relationships, most often it's within the context of a single issue, such as drug or alcohol use. But while those studies are helpful, they don't tackle these critical relationships head on. Far too little is known about the unique characteristics of peer friendships when applied solely to midadolescents. Yet it is during this period that peer relations take on an extremely significant role in the life of young people.

We will examine four aspects of clusters that are vital in seeking to understand how adolescents experience, define, and order their world:

1. Why clusters are created
2. The key characteristics of clusters

3. How clusters form and evolve

4. How cluster members relate to one another

Why Clusters Are Created

Generally peer relationships have been seen as a normal part of the adolescent process. They address the need to belong and they provide a cohesive unit that serves as glue for society. An even more significant driving force for clustering today is the need for young people to find a safe place where they can simply *be*.

Parents have gradually pushed aside their children to the point that kids feel they have no choice but to form intimate associations with peers to replace what has been lost at home. They hunger for a place where there is no danger of being ignored, used, or pushed aside.

Clusters develop because midadolescents know they have no choice but to find a safe, supportive family and community, and in a culture of abandonment, the peer group seems to be the only option they have.

The Key Characteristics of Clusters

A cluster is a group of adolescents who identify themselves as a defined relational unit. Adolescents don't use the word *cluster*, but they cluster nonetheless, typically describing members of their own clusters as their "friends." But no matter what they're called, clusters have the following distinguishing characteristics.

- *Size*. Clusters can contain as few as four or five members and as many as eight or ten (rarely more) members.
- *Gender*. Clusters are almost always gender specific. But often a male cluster will align itself with a female cluster and the two will spend a great deal of time together.
- *Timing*. Typically, joining a cluster is a significant waypoint on the journey into midadolescence. In most cases this happens sometime during the latter months of the freshman year and is often solidified by the end of the sophomore year. Often these cluster attachments last until late adolescence, when youth begin to broaden their experiences and social networks

70

through work, college, or military service. For those who stay in their hometown or go to a nearby college and remain devoted to their cluster, the power of the cluster can cause them to remain in midadolescence for several years.

- *Loyalty and commitment*. A cluster is familial in that once it is formed, there is a strong implicit agreement to remain loyal.
- *Rules and norms*. While a cluster is being developed, a subtle, almost imperceptible negotiation goes on among the members. The necessary rules, norms, values, and even narratives

Youth Culture Update

"Not Just Shaking Your Booty"

It's not just the same old grind in Argyle, Texas. In fact "grinding"—the provocative, hip-hop–inspired form of dance—has been banned from the local high school by superintendent Jason Ceyanes. "This is not just shaking your booty," he said. "This is pelvis-to-pelvis physical contact in the private areas . . . and then moving around."

Students are less than thrilled with the ban, and many parents have jumped to the defense of their kids. Some were so incensed that they started anti-Ceyanes blogs, dishing that the superintendent fathered a child at age seventeen. Ceyanes's supporters struck back. One posted pictures of students in suggestive clothing—pulled directly from the students' MySpace or Facebook sites—with the suggestion the "little angels" (as the blogger wrote) could use a little dancehall restraint. The post was later removed.

Ceyanes, meanwhile, has enlisted the help of local dance instructors to help teach kids what's appropriate boogie behavior for a high school dance. But some dance experts fear it's a lost cause. "If you're dancing to a song that says 'shake that, shake that, shake that,' it's kind of hard not to shake that," said Dallas choreographer Gino Johnson.

71

of the cluster that serve to bind the members together are all worked out prior to the cluster's ultimate formation. After these have been established, members tend to subordinate their own personal convictions, loyalties, and norms to the will of the collective whole.

How Clusters Form and Evolve

There has been little research explaining why teenagers choose the friends they do, especially during midadolescence, when clustering takes place. But one thing is clear: kids cluster with other kids who are similar to themselves.

As emerging midadolescents begin to realize that they need friends to have a home base from which to navigate their psychosocial journey, they see the path of least resistance as the most important factor in determining their friendship cluster. Most students remain close to their natural affinity groups even while they search for friendships outside those groups.

What role do parents play in their children's cluster formation? While adults would like to think that parents' values and preferences would play a role in their kids' peer groups, it is clear to me that the key factor for today's abandoned teens is finding friends who will provide a sense of comfort and safety.

Most students say their parents were not involved in helping to choose their group, while some said that their parents were actually opposed to their choice of friends. Experience suggests that the role parents play in their children's social lives is based on the quality of the relationship that children and parents have with each other. One of the most important aspects of this parental relationship is whether or not it builds or destroys the adolescent's sense of self-confidence, which is the most important force in shaping the formation of clusters.

Cluster formation and development are also influenced by a young person's age and emotional maturity, which are changing rapidly during the middle school and high school years. The kids I talked to indicated they were aware of some of these changes:

- "My friends from junior high are different now. It's like everybody is changing."

72

- "I'm not the same person I was last year. And my friends, well, they just don't seem to do it for me, you know?"
- "I don't feel as close to my friends as I did last year. We promised we'd stay close, but now we're kinda drifting apart."

Social Clusters and the Journey from Childhood to Adulthood

As young people make the sometimes traumatic transition from early adolescence to midadolescence, clusters play an increasingly important role. As young people enter high school and ultimately begin to recognize that life is going to be different for them from this point forward, they look at their friends in new ways. At the same time, young people are on a bigger journey to adulthood. During this journey, children realize that they must begin to separate from their family and established family roles to become unique and individualized people.

Adolescence is a fifteen-year psychosocial journey of self-discovery and self-acceptance that is, at times, a treacherous experience. No matter where adolescents are on this journey, they feel somewhat lost as they move away from the securities of family to new clusters and communities they discover at school and elsewhere.

For midadolescents, the emotional and relational antidote to feeling that they are in a no-man's-land is found in the protection of intimate peer relationships. During this time, friends attain heightened significance as the only support system believed to be both authentically committed and readily available.

Development of Self-Concept

I observed that students choose their clusters based on their self-concept. In turn, clusters play a powerful role in shaping their self-concept. For example, if a student attempts to build a deep and meaningful friendship with someone who holds a healthier self-concept, that student will constantly feel inferior, thus negating the reason for clustering in the first place. If, however, a student attempts to build a cluster with someone who has a lower self-concept than he or she, that person will feel as though he or she is

73

Small Groups as Clusters to Offer Security

Vern Hill

As a middle-aged youth worker with thirty-five years of experience, the effect of *Hurt* on my work was similar to the effect of cataract surgery on clouded eyesight. I was able to wipe away decades of collected residue of what was assumed about youth and see clearly and realistically the current state of the young people I know and love.

Hurt identified and verbalized much of what I was experiencing with young people but was unable to comprehend. The freedom of seeing kids for who they actually are has given me insight, confidence, and direction for the important time I spend with the young people I serve.

Most helpful to me was learning about clusters and how they impact young people in midadolescence. Seeing, in a new way, young people's increased need to find a "safe place" encouraged me to instill a sense of security in our programs and messages. Realizing the depth of desire for intimacy that drives this need for clustering today, I sought new avenues to create depth in our small groups. Knowing the role of the cluster as a familial grouping (and the inherent advantages and disadvantages of such) moved me to be more diligent in providing the young people we serve with clear information about life issues, guidance about personal ethics, and training in life skills.

The insight and clarity about clusters that *Hurt* provided gave me voice and vocabulary to engage others to be better equipped to serve the young people in our community. Our staff and leaders discussed the validity of the concept and embraced

being socially and emotionally dragged down by the person with the lower self-concept.

Of course most kids don't realize they are desperately searching for a safe social place through clusters. But whether they realize it or not, the dance of cluster formation is a highly complex process of relational exploration and negotiation.

I was surprised to witness the power of clusters in the lives of today's teens. They depend heavily on them for rules, norms, and expectations. This is a time of rethinking previously held commitments and assumptions. The primary concern of the vast majority of adolescents is finding common ground with their newly aligned cluster. Previously held convictions are latently present, but pleasing the cluster is more important than holding on to these convictions.

the reality of clusters. We went on to design and modify our ministry to reflect the opportunities clusters present.

Educating parents through discussions proved particularly fruitful. One "brown-bag lunch" on the topic drew thirty parents who expressed not only their affirmation of the reality of clusters in their children's lives but a heartfelt appreciation for the illumination the concept brought to their desire to be better parents. One parent began to provide weekly meals and desserts for their child's cluster as a way to empower a healthy setting for the cluster and initiate a supportive relationship.

One especially satisfying result was the positive response from the youth-serving professionals in our community. When presented with the information, youth ministers readily accepted the concept as a reality and integrated the belief into their assumptions about youth. A local psychologist who works primarily with youth listened, studied, and used the idea of clusters to inform her therapeutic work with kids. I was most encouraged that teachers, both new and veteran, saw the concept as a revelation in their understanding of youth culture. Using the topic of clusters as a starting point to discuss today's youth provided a more accurate way of understanding our community's young people. This led to program changes and modifications that allow us to better serve the young people around us.

Chief among the changes we made was the drive to recruit more leaders for our programs. The emphasis for our leaders focused less on what we do and more on building relationships with young people. In short, we wanted more leaders to concentrate on a smaller number of young people. As we plan for camps and retreats, we set up our

This all takes place beneath the conscious awareness of the adolescent. Clusters are subconsciously chosen according to who will make one feel the most welcome and safe with the least amount of work and stress, even though this is rarely if ever verbalized.

How Cluster Members Relate to One Another

Clusters are the building blocks on which adolescent society is built. Thick walls develop around clusters as they create a series of social and operational rules and norms. Each cluster functions as an independent unit with its own approved behaviors, which continually reinforce the predetermined values of the cluster. Yet some cluster members have self-concepts similar to those in other clusters, so they create bonds of friendship that extend beyond the

cabin groups with clusters in mind. Operating from this new perspective has made clear the need for a 1:4 ratio of leaders to youth instead of the 1:8 ratio we had been using.

The bulk of our programs shifted from large-group to small-group formats. The large group, it seems, has become less relevant. Small groups, especially those approximating the size of a cluster, are gaining strength and significance. Young people have appreciated our shift to being more direct as we deal with life issues, life skills, and ethics. These are topics clusters seem ill equipped to address.

The most empowering feature the cluster concept brought to our programming is the clear indication that kids are desperate to experience the grace, intimacy, and community that Jesus offers. Increasingly our messages stress the security that is provided through life in the body of Christ. In our talks and relationships we expose kids to the forgiveness and acceptance Jesus demonstrates. Constantly we explain and describe the close, personal, and deeply intimate love that only Jesus can offer.

Because of *Hurt*, I can clearly see the forces that affect the lives of the kids I serve. The confidence, freedom, and energy I've gained from this unobstructed vision have helped countless young people in my program and other programs in our community.

Vern Hill, with a master's degree in counseling and theology, is Area Director for Young Life in Stillwater, Minnesota. He has thirty-five years of experience working with young people. Vern supervises many diverse programs, including Young Life "clubs," support groups for teens with abuse and addiction needs, tutoring programs for at-risk youth, teen mom programs, and ethical leadership programs. Go to stillwater.younglife.org.

cluster boundaries. Andy Root, a seminary student of mine, calls these "cousin clusters."

At the same time, individuals within clusters may develop a hostile view toward those in clusters with different social views. In its most extreme case, this hostility can result in violence or even death, as in the case of the Columbine High School shootings. In this case, members of an ostracized group known as the "trench coat mafia" killed members of other clusters.

In my research I observed definite rules and boundaries between cousin clusters. These rules governed where students hung out before school, whom they sat with at lunch, which hallways they walked down, whom they talked to in class, and even what events they attended.

Some students can overcome the social barriers that separate students from different clusters by "being friends" in a specific and ordered context (such as on a sports team). But the majority of the time, clusters set up extremely subtle but clearly delineated "demilitarized zones," and all parties tacitly understand that they will not get involved with one another.

Clusters have replaced cliques, but they haven't done away with the undercurrent of stratification, hostility, and even potential violence that seem to be a perennial reality of midadolescent social life.

Our Way or Their Way?

The thing I find most interesting about clusters is how thoroughly this phenomenon affects the student community. In fact, in the high schools I have visited, there is no longer any such thing as a "student community."

Unfortunately, the adults who are trying to reach and help teens have not awakened to this new social reality. To the contrary, all the services and systems that churches, social workers, the therapeutic community, and others have developed to serve midadolescents are lost in a time warp that assumes some kind of cohesive school community, but this kind of community is rapidly vanishing or already long gone.

Coaches still rely on students' willingness and ability to work as a team, with mixed success. And in the world of Christian youth work, churches and parachurch organizations try to bring young people from a wide variety of schools and clusters into big groups they call fellowship. Adults' intentions may be good, but their assumptions about teens' social lives are outmoded. Therefore the programs and services they devise to serve kids do not adequately address the changes in how youth relate to one another. As a result, young people are once again offered up on the altar of an adult agenda at the cost of their personal sense of safety.

Let me state it more plainly. Many times today's teenagers are thrown together in false relationships by well-meaning adults who think kids connect with one another just like they used to in the good old days. Most teens will try to cooperate with adults by fulfilling the ill-fitting roles we have assigned them. This outward obedience and conformity will ultimately fail to reach kids where they are, because, for many teens, how they appear on the outside is far different from the driving sense of place and home they crave on the inside.

Connecting with Kids

Clusters are not necessarily good or bad. They can be either. But most of the time they just *are*. They are the way young people connect today, as opposed to the cliques of an earlier generation. Those adults who understand this will be better prepared to care for teens in ways that make a real impact.

Although clusters may be short-term arrangements, they nonetheless provide a sense of connection, rootedness, and family for young people who desperately hunger for these things. Rather than criticizing, adults should find ways to honor and connect to the clusters of the young people they love. I have found that once an adult is "in" with a member of a cluster, he or she is soon "in" with everyone else.

Most important, we need to realize that the intense loyalty and commitment young people exhibit toward their clusters are manifestations of their quest to fill the gaping holes in their hearts that are caused by their sense of abandonment. Even while operating in intimate and exclusive social relationships, today's kids are still lonely. Somehow the cluster is not all it is advertised to be. Should we expose this vulnerability? I don't think so. Rather we should seek ways to play a greater role in kids' lives by simply being there for them. Instead of proclaiming our agenda or giving kids our list of critiques of their world, we should come alongside them and help them find the safety net they are seeking through their clusters.

5

school daze

We all have our memories of school and the various teachers we had over the years. Some teachers inspired and encouraged us. Some bored us out of our skulls.

When I was back in a public school classroom once again, I got a closer look at the world of today's kids. Unfortunately, I wound up teaching alongside one of the world's worst teachers.

She had been teaching for a decade but had never learned even the most basic notions of respect. She used the most flippant and callous language to put down her students, some of whom I knew personally. Why couldn't she see in these young people the potential I saw in them? Why did she respond to their imperfect classroom behavior or academic performance by dismissing their ability to ever produce anything of value? I have been working among teenagers for three decades, so I have heard countless stories about unfeeling, unfair teachers, but suddenly I was seeing a teacher who made all these stories seem overly positive!

Teachers are people, and whether people are teachers or youth workers (or even authors!), there are good apples and bad apples. Over my years of work with young people, I have tended to see things from the teacher's perspective, but my eyes were opened to some of what kids had been telling me. There are some great teachers, but on the other hand, some teachers apparently never had the ability to teach or they lost the ability somewhere along the way or they completely forgot what originally inspired them to choose this important line of work.

Of course I sympathize with educators, including teachers and counselors. My experience is that many of these people are professional and well intentioned but they have become overwhelmed with the demands of their job, fed up with the constant criticism they receive, and discouraged by the many students who don't seem to care much about anything. Some teachers seem to have locked themselves into a bubble that protects them as they go about their daily activities and duties.

These problems have been documented by writers like Denise Clark Pope, author of *Doing School: How We Are Creating a Generation of Stressed Out, Materialistic, and Miseducated Students*, who wrote: "Instead of fostering in its students traits of honesty, integrity, cooperation, and respect, the school may be promoting deception, hostility, and anxiety."

Teaching is a tough but high calling—one that demands flexibility, openness, constant retooling, and the kind of temperament and psychological health that can handle student, parental, and administrative critique as well as a lack of motivation and even disrespect from midadolescents.

It's a Blackboard Jungle Out There

Quick, what's on your list of favorite movies about high school? Are you picturing the idealistic teacher Sidney Poitier in 1967's *To Sir, With Love* or the nihilistic and sexually adventurous girls in 2003's *Thirteen*?

High school has become a pop-culture icon because its elements (proms, homecoming, football games, lunchroom, pop quizzes, cheerleaders, school plays, nerds/geeks/freaks, letter jackets, dances, parties, and yearbooks) bring back a flood of memories for every adult.

In many cases the high school years are portrayed as the best years of one's life, but for a great many contemporary students, high school is not too thrilling. When one student I knew heard

80

the "best years of your life" refrain, she was shocked. "Great!" she exclaimed. "If this is the best it's ever going to get, I might as well kill myself now!"

I understood her feelings as I walked the hallways with her and other teens. Our culture has changed and so have our schools. And as I saw during my recent return to the classroom, the school days many adults remember have been replaced by a brave and sometimes disturbing new world.

Let's take a fresh look at today's schools, first through the eyes of teachers and then through the eyes of teens.

The View from the Podium

Many of today's teachers have it tough, and I observed that most are doing a good job under a rigid, politically driven, difficult system. America's educational system places many layers of expectations and demands on teachers and administrators, and often what society asks of them is not fair. They are poorly paid, lack sufficient resources, could use additional training and encouragement, and are overloaded with the demands made on them by classroom size, the rigors of objectified test scores, and a difficult cultural world. They get little thanks and are constantly under the microscope of parents and administrators. It's little wonder many are discouraged.

What may be more surprising is that many remain committed to their work, which was one of the four lessons I learned as I sought to see things from the teachers' point of view.

1. Teachers Believe in Learning

Most of the teachers I saw believe that learning is (or at least should be) a pleasurable experience and that the ultimate goal of learning (and thus teaching) is the joy it produces.

Research has taught us some things about the effectiveness of teachers. Consistently it shows that teachers who are passionate about their subjects are more effective teachers. Likewise, teachers who genuinely like students have greater success at encouraging students to excel. As a result, the teacher (counselor, youth worker, or coach) who has a passion for both the subject matter and the students is by far the most effective.

81

Failing Grades

Schools in some of the country's largest cities are struggling to graduate their students, according to a new report. The report, issued by America's Promise Alliance, found that schools in Detroit, Indianapolis, Cleveland, and fourteen other major U.S. cities graduated only 50 percent of their students.

About 70 percent of American youth graduate on time overall. That means about 1.2 million students drop out before graduation—far too many for Colin Powell, the former secretary of state and the Alliance's founding chair. "When more than one million students a year drop out of high school, it's more than a problem, it's a catastrophe," he says.

But the catastrophe is most apparent in major urban areas. Detroit's public schools graduate just 24.9 percent of their students. In Indianapolis only 30.5 percent of students get their diplomas. The spread between urban and suburban schools in some of those underperforming cities is even more striking. Baltimore's suburban schools graduate 81.5 percent of their students. In urban Baltimore, the graduation rate drops to 34.6 percent.

We also know that teachers who help their students connect the dots between the subject matter and its life application are able to relate to students on a deeper level. Students who find something they can latch onto in classes like chemistry, algebra, or English literature will work harder. Other students find room in the curriculum for things they already enjoy, such as sports, drama, or student government.

But sometimes teachers who believe learning should be a pleasurable experience fail to realize the degree to which school bores many students out of their minds. Instead of enjoying school, most kids merely say it is okay. And often the difference in the opinions of students and of teachers about school drives a wedge of misunderstanding between them. I could see this in the way that many students believed their teachers were disappointed in and critical of them.

Students wanted teachers to appreciate them and not to hold anything against them, but few teachers I talked to could grasp this. This difference in perspective is one of the biggest factors in the failure of today's schools.

2. Teachers Pigeonhole Students

I also saw that many teachers make snap judgments about students that hinder kids' ability to grow and develop. I believe some teachers may actually be doing more harm than good, as I saw when I attended an annual banquet for a varsity sports team.

As the coach summoned each student athlete forward for recognition, it was clear from his comments that he valued the contributions of some but considered others too inconsequential for any real respect. Some students were praised, while others were ignored or explicitly disparaged.

When I asked other coaches and parents about what I was seeing, the most common response was, "Oh, that's just how Coach is." Some even lauded him for his rudeness, saying, "Coach doesn't pull any punches. These kids have to learn how to handle the truth!"

If we want our schools to teach that some kids are worthy and some are junk, then this school is succeeding. But for so many kids who have bad relationships with teachers, school becomes little more than a game. During this phase of development, students live out their "school self" as they operate within the school's expectations and parameters of conduct. This includes the persona they reflect and the relationships they initiate with their teachers.

For many teachers, the litmus test of a "good" student is how much respect the student shows. But students no longer grant respect to teachers automatically. Instead, they feel their respect must be earned. No wonder many teachers feel what seems like disdain from their students.

3. Teachers Feel Beat Up

A significant number of teachers feel overwhelmed by the challenge of teaching in today's public school system. Most feel under-appreciated and even abused by their administration, district, and state. One recent report found that teachers felt "their views are generally ignored by decision makers, with 70 percent feeling left out of the loop in their district's decision-making process."

Along with budgetary woes, this was the leading complaint I heard from teachers. This discouragement is sometimes reflected in a negative attitude that spills over into the classroom and onto the individual psyches of the students they have committed themselves to serve.

Researchers have suggested that teachers play a more important role in furthering the developmental trajectory of adolescents than they do teaching them a particular subject area. Many teachers recognize this, and yet the demands of standardized testing, score-based evaluation systems, behavior problems, and a host of other factors all cause teachers to feel stretched beyond their ability. Add to this the pressure that teachers represent one of the last remaining *institutions* that cares for these adolescents, and it's little wonder that teachers are discouraged.

4. Teachers Don't Know What to Do about Parents

Teachers told me they'd love more help from parents, but parents are less and less involved with high schools. And while most teachers publicly bemoan the lack of parental involvement, some teachers see parents as a threat. The parent-teacher relationship is one of the more complex and at times stressful relationships in the overall high school structure.

Teachers believe that children are far more successful when their parents are involved with both the student and the school. At the same time, teachers feel on a regular basis as though parents are more interested in defending their children and rationalizing their behavior and performance than in allowing teachers to offer their expertise in solving problems.

In my experience, teachers are often scared of parents. This fear may unintentionally convey, usually in the first few minutes of a conference or a phone conversation, that the teacher is not interested in a parent's perspective. Add to this dynamic the parents' own fears—fears that they have far less control over their child than they are supposed to have (and that the school is often the

84

The Wrong Kind of "High" School

Teens say drug problems are growing in their schools, and parents wonder just how much they can do about it.

According to a study by Columbia University's National Center on Addiction and Substance Abuse, 61 percent of high school teens say their high school has a drug problem, compared with 44 percent who said the same thing in 2002. Problems are rising in middle schools, too, with 31 percent of middle schoolers saying their school has drug issues. That's up from 19 percent five years ago.

About six of every ten parents polled said it was unrealistic to expect their children's schools to be drug free.

instigator, or at least a breeding ground, for their kids' problems). These issues place a significant wedge between a parent and a high school teacher even before they talk.

In numerous conversations with teachers and administrators, I found that the problem may lie with teacher training, which tells them they are the only societal institution left that has the education, training, and commitment to understand and nurture the young. Unfortunately, this attitude alienates parents and families. While educators believe overwhelmingly in the necessity of parental involvement, some are critical of anyone who lacks a teacher's narrow perspective and focus.

As I talked to teachers and parents I saw that most parents are concerned about their children's education, even if it is not their highest priority. In addition, parents have to worry about their kids' sexual behavior, the Internet and the media, the impact of clustering and peers, and the constant temptation of substance abuse.

A high school teacher sees a student for less than an hour a day, and for the most part, that teacher's entire perception of the student is based on the external roles, behavior, and academic performance shown during that hour. A teacher almost never knows anything

85

about the dynamics of the family system of the student, their friendships, internal struggles, or how other adults perceive them. For this reason, it is unfortunate that some teachers make snap judgments about students, which both students and parents are forced to live with until the end of the semester or even longer.

The View from the Desk

It was easy for me to get students to open up and discuss how they feel about school, and their views were varied and diverse. Some students were serious about their studies. Some did just the minimum to get by. And others did not seem to care at all. But there were four major themes that emerged as I talked to kids about school.

1. Students Say Respect Must Be Earned

Most adolescents say that teachers do not deserve respect simply because they are teachers. In fact most students don't believe that teachers even deserve the benefit of the doubt and must earn respect by first showing respect to students. This attitude breaks a previously unchallenged value of our culture—that older people deserve respect and kindness from younger people, unless older people do something to nullify that expectation. Adults can complain about this shift, but if we want to be effective, we need to deal with it.

2. Students Care about Grades but Not Necessarily Learning

Students approach academic achievement differently than do the adults in their lives, as David Brooks pointed out in the *Weekly Standard*:

> One of the most destructive forces in American life today is the tyranny of the grade point average. Everyone argues about whether SATs are an unjust measure of student ability, but the GPA does far more harm. To get into top schools, students need to get straight A's or close. That means that students are not rewarded for developing a passion for a subject and following their curiosity wherever it takes them. . . . They are rewarded for mastering the method of being a good student, not for their passion for the content of any particular area of learning. They are rewarded for their ability to

86

mindlessly defer to their professors' wishes, and never strike out on their own or follow a contradictory path.

There are some teens who love learning for the sake of learning, but most kids I talked to could articulate little more than a powerful personal drive and agenda to "get somewhere" when it came to academic achievement. The days of a high school student finding learning to be a pleasurable experience rather than a means to an end are all but gone, yet some adults continue to perpetuate an ideal of learning as an inherent good.

A student will do whatever it takes to navigate the complex and varied demands of midadolescence with as much self-protection and self-interest as necessary. Students who believe that getting good grades helps them feel better about themselves do what they have to do to get those grades. For those whose primary strategies lie outside the classroom, grades are less important. What seems to be nearly universal is that the high school system forces many midadolescents to do whatever it takes—cheat, plagiarize, or download—to get good grades on tests and papers.

High school students are also confused about college. Very few students know precisely what they want in the future or why. Most try to maintain grades and relatively stable relationships with teachers because it suits their idea of how best to survive high school, not because it is a step toward a career or college.

3. Most Students Cheat

Cheating is so widespread on high school campuses that it is considered by many to be the norm. Cheating for midadolescents is a complex issue, thanks to mixed messages from parents and schools, the lack of a clear and universal definition of academic dishonesty, and the widespread relativism of society. Many simply do what is necessary to fulfill the expectations of the academic role they are playing.

To midadolescents, cheating is rarely considered a moral problem, but when it is, cheating students rarely see themselves as the culprits. Rather, they are unfortunate victims who had no other option.

Today two rigid ethical commitments crash into one another at both the high school and the college level: the traditional ethic of academic integrity and the contemporary adolescent perspective that cheating is an acceptable and even relatively moral option for the student who needs to perform well. This is an even bigger problem when one realizes that, in one way or another, at one time or another, virtually everyone cheats.

The most frequent reason students give for cheating is the injustice of teachers. If a teacher were fairer, the argument goes, there would be little need to cheat. In dozens of conversations with students regarding cheating, the closest I got to anyone recognizing that cheating was a moral problem was when a girl told me about a boy who cheated regularly by copying from her tests. He "didn't care at all about studying," and he was therefore taking advantage of her. The fact that he cheated was not the problem: She was morally outraged because he had used *her* papers to cheat.

Adults have created a world in which adolescents accept that deceit is a viable way to succeed. As Denise Clark Pope points out, "Successful students learned to devise various strategies to stay ahead of their peers and to please those in power positions; unsuccessful students, for a variety of reasons, were not as adept at playing the survival game."

This "game" has produced a continuum of students who range from those who are proficient at conforming to others' expectations to those who must figure out how to survive when they cannot live up to those expectations. Midadolescents learn to cope, indeed, to survive, without adults, or adult rules of conduct.

4. Students Are Anxious about School

Students who care about grades and academic performance are experiencing an ever-increasing level of anxiety and stress over school. Two elements that add to the stress level of these students are the increasing amount of homework required and the university-mandated need to be involved in as many activities as possible.

The school in which I conducted my research expected each student to spend from forty-five minutes to an hour per day on homework for each class. Students are required to take five classes, meaning that each weeknight they could legitimately spend more than three hours doing homework.

In addition to this academic requirement many students are required (by parents or others) to be involved in athletics (two to three or more hours per day) and extracurricular activities and clubs (such as school-based Key Club, faith-based Young Life, or a church youth group). And on top of all that, there is often an expectation to put in volunteer hours.

For many "good students," the day starts before 7 a.m. They get home after practice or a meeting at 5 or 6 p.m., do an hour of homework, grab dinner before heading out to an activity, get home at 9:30 or 10, and finish homework around 1 a.m.

The majority of the students I observed, especially those who were active and involved, were often exhausted and frazzled. Adults seemed to give little thought to considering what these schedules, expectations, and pressures do to the development and health of midadolescents.

Growing Up or Scamming the System?

My return to school introduced me to a world where students feel anonymous and powerless. Many students had learned at an early age how to "play to" the expectations of the system, yet doing so separated them from authentic engagement with that very system and its reason for being.

Some researchers try to put a positive spin on this, arguing that adolescents who navigate the complex process of going to school and growing up are learning to accumulate "social capital." By working to fulfill others' expectations, they are supposedly growing up. But I fear this is a catch-22 for adolescents. The successful students are those who are able to play the game better than their less successful peers. They are not actually being nurtured and assimilated into the adult world by caring mentors; they are learning how to scam the system.

Sadly, my return to school forced me to conclude that what happens on high school campuses in many ways hurts our young. So what can we do about it? I have one recommendation concerning teachers and one concerning students.

As for teachers, we need to reward the ones who actually help kids grow and develop while assisting those who should not be in a classroom to find another line of work. When I talked to one award-winning teacher, he said there was no big mystery to his success: "It's the same thing it takes to be a great spouse or parent or coach or leader in any setting. It's not mystical and it sure isn't a secret. It is just caring enough for each person in front of you that they know they matter to you. To be a great teacher means I am allowed the privilege of being with great kids."

As for students, we need to get rid of the one-size-fits-all approach we have adopted in the majority of our public schools. One obvious problem is that the timing of development is different for each person, and development has a direct impact on such things as cognitive memory and recall. Surviving, much less thriving, in early and midadolescence requires the ability to juggle multiple classes and all their educational and relational demands for fifty minutes at a time. A student who is even slightly behind developmentally is put at a severe disadvantage in the rigid, tightly controlled educational environment of the American high school.

There is also strong evidence that both learning and intelligence are extremely complex processes and that there are multiple types of intelligences. For example, one can be book smart or street smart. We need to recognize that young people are the most precious and fragile resources of our society. Each one has a unique potential that needs a deliberate, proactive, and nurturing school environment.

I agree with Mel Levine, the author of *A Mind at a Time*, when he says that every adolescent is, by definition, in a state of transition and growth and therefore needs individual attention in every aspect of their lives, including education.

This is a tall order for a teacher who has five classes of thirty students each, but we do not have the luxury of thinking of students as "classes" or of putting them in boxes with labels such as "average," "gifted," and "obnoxious." Each young person has tremendous potential within the context of his or her unique giftedness and therefore deserves personal care, attention, and a system that seeks individual growth and development.

6

fractured family values

For years, millions of Americans tuned their TVs to watch Art Linkletter, one of the most beloved entertainers in history. Between 1998 and 2000 he hosted a popular CBS show with Bill Cosby called *Kids Say the Darndest Things* in which the hosts would ask children questions and await their humorous responses. The show, which spawned copycat shows in England and Australia, also generated a series of Linkletter books called *Kids Say the Darndest Things*.

Linkletter's viewers and readers couldn't get enough of the cute things kids would blurt out when they opened up and said what was on their mind. But recently I was shocked when I was talking to a group of young people and one of them opened up and told me about his family. What he had to say was not cute.

"Okay," said Jeremy, a high school junior who had been sitting silently during a talk I was giving to a group of high school youth. "I'll tell you something I've never told an adult. In fact I'll tell you something I've never told anybody. Three years ago my parents got divorced and they decided to keep it a secret. They told me and my sister that we weren't allowed to tell anyone, not even our grandparents, or we would get in big trouble. So for three years we all have been living a lie. I haven't told my friends, my coaches, my teachers, nobody, and neither has my little sister. My parents hate each other, and they fight all the time, but they pretend to be happily married around everyone else. It sucks!"

I tried not to look shocked but I was. I felt certain Jeremy's situation was one in a million, or one in a billion. I prepared to move on to another topic. Then the shy, young girl on my left let me know that Jeremy was not alone. "Me, too," she said quietly as she bit her nails and squirmed.

"Excuse me?" I said.

"Okay, I guess it doesn't matter anymore anyway. My parents did the same thing to us last year. I hate them! I hate them both!"

As I desperately tried to gather myself and say something coherent, the school bell rang, and the kids I had been talking with scattered in a dozen different directions. I had been saved by the bell.

Kids *do* say the darndest things, but the things today's kids say about their families are a far cry from the *Happy Days* image that Linkletter offered up. There are times when each one of us would prefer to live in a fantasyland of the imagination rather than face the tragic truths many kids live day after day. But if we wish to help our young people, we need to listen to them and understand them first.

I knew families were under intense pressure long before I met these kids, but the depressing stories I heard showed me that the

Youth Culture Update

Bad Start

About one of every fifty babies in the United States has been neglected or abused, and about a third of those infants were a week old or less when the maltreatment took place. The government says that more than ninety-one thousand infants were victimized between October 1, 2005, and September 30, 2006. About 70 percent of these children were neglected, which includes things like abandonment and newborn drug addiction—"not things like parents learning how to be parents," according to Rebecca Leeb of the Centers for Disease Control and Prevention.

brokenness in today's families is far more pervasive and destructive than I had ever imagined.

We've all seen the stories about how kids are affected by divorce, blended families, parents' financial pressures, and the rapid pace of life. And any of us who have worked with kids have seen the ripple effect of these problems in young people's emotional and psychological distress.

In this chapter we'll look at today's fractured family values and explore ways we can help kids who are caught up in the turmoil.

Fighting over the Family

Type the word *family* into the Google search engine and in under a second you'll get more than 850 million web matches. Obviously this is a subject that matters a great deal to many people. The problem is that we can't seem to agree on what a family is.

Many Americans would accept the United States Census Bureau's definition: "two or more persons related by birth, marriage, or adoption who reside in the same household."

But a 2002 study published by the American Psychological Association found that there is no longer any standard definition of family. "Families today can take many forms—single parent, shared custody, adoptive, blended, foster, traditional dual parent, to name a few," said Andrea Solarz, the study's author.

During the last quarter century, there has been a culture war over the definition of *family*. On one side are "conservative" activists who seek to rouse public support and enact legislative measures to support and preserve traditional models of the nuclear family. On the other side are "liberal" activists, like a professor I worked with during my doctoral studies, who want to expand the definition to include same-sex couples and other groups.

There have been victories and losses for each side, but as the battle continues, it seems clear that the greatest casualties of this culture war have been our children. While adults have battled over definitions and legislation, children have suffered widespread abandonment.

Here's what *family* means to some of the young people I have talked with:

First Comes Love, Then Comes the Baby . . .

Nearly four in ten babies were born out of wedlock in 2005, according to government health statistics. That's a record, and a surprising one at that, considering the teen pregnancy rate hit an all-time low.

Experts say the increase has more to do with twenty-something couples living together longer and putting off marriage until after they have children.

- Geri lived with her little sister and mother and her mother's latest boyfriend in his house with his three kids (when they were not at their mother's). Her family was her mother, sister, and the boyfriend (but not his kids).
- Kim says she does not have a family. She never met her birth father. And the man who acts as her father is her mother's former boyfriend. She doesn't refer to him as Dad but calls him by his first name.
- For Kara, *family* means maternal grandparents, aunts, and uncles. Meanwhile, she lives with a shifting cast of characters that includes her birth mother, an older sister and her boyfriend, and another man who is the grandfather of one of her closest friends.
- For Greg, *family* is a word used at Thanksgiving and Christmastime. Greg lives with his mom, who has been divorced twice. They live next door to Mom's boyfriend, a man Greg is forced to call Dad. Greg is angry because he believes his mother pushed his birth father out of their lives.
- Sam has two moms and no dad.

From the dawn of human history, families have nurtured and trained the young. And a growing library of social scientific research finds that the best and safest families are those where children are loved and cared for by a supportive mother and father. This doesn't mean that a family has to be sitcom perfect like *Leave It to Beaver*, or that single-parent families can't be supportive. But the research clearly shows that kids who grow up with the safety and security of a relationally committed father and mother have a better chance of growing up knowing they are unconditionally accepted and loved.

On the other hand, family environments that are unsafe or unloving are more likely to produce young people who struggle with self-concept, sexual acting out, substance abuse, and difficulties trusting friends or authority figures.

My own work with teens has confirmed that kids who are sexually "loose" often come from families with absentee fathers. Those who use their bodies to find comfort and connection through sexual play are trying to prove to themselves and to the world that they are worthy of love. In other words, those who are the most desperate for affection are not receiving it at home. (This is true of both boys and girls, but the behavior and attitudes of girls has drawn more attention.)

The harmful effects of flawed families are not limited to external behaviors, such as sexuality, substance abuse, or partying. They also show themselves in negative attitudes, lack of confidence, and brokenness in other aspects of life.

Functioning families are crucial for the development of adolescents, but our society's experiments in fractured family values hurt more than our young people. They impact our entire society.

Facts versus Fiction

What would happen if we were to read each and every one of the 350 million Google hits on parenting? Would this help us as parents know how to parent better?

Let me save you some time. Here are the indisputable facts about parenting that have been affirmed by both the social sciences and my own work with kids.

Parenting Is Work

I've shared with you some of the things young people tell me about their experience of family. I've also talked to plenty of par-

Being Present in the Midst of Our Teens' Pain

Derwin L. Gray

Have you ever encountered someone who tattoos your soul? Following my morning sermon at a summer youth camp, a brunette, sixteen-year-old girl with sad eyes, whom I call Sammie (not her real name), asked if I would talk with her at lunch. She told me how she was beaten by her biological mother, sexually abused by her stepfather, and told by her biological father that she was worthless. To cope with her pain, she sliced up her arms with razors; she even shoved nails in her ears.

In Sammie I experienced authenticity. Tenderly she asked me, "Where was God when I was being beaten by my mom? Where was God when I was being sexually abused? Where is God now that I have been abandoned by my parents?"

I shared with her that our God is not absent from our pain; he is forever present in our pain and at the cross he suffered along with us.

Sammie said, "D. Gray, thank you for listening. No Christian has ever listened to me like you have. I'm not a Christian, but you have helped me move a step closer to becoming one."

At the conclusion of my evening sermon, teens flooded the stage in response to Jesus's offer of life. Among them I saw Sammie with tears streaming down her face. May her tears be symbolic of God's healing grace falling on her soul.

Derwin L. Gray, "The Evangelism Linebacker," is Vicki's husband, Presley and Jeremiah's papa; he is Pastor of Preaching and Discipleship at theGathering (www.thegatheringnc.org), and president of One Heart At A Time Ministries (www.oneheartatatime.org).

ents, and the main message that comes through loud and clear is that many parents' own lives are so fragmented and broken they don't have the time, energy, or commitment to work at being good parents.

Our world is not overflowing with happy and healthy moms and dads who are trying to make life miserable for their kids. Instead, it seems that moms and dads themselves are struggling to keep their fast-paced, overstressed, disjointed lives together. When that doesn't work, it's often the kids who suffer the consequences.

One of the main things I hear from teens is a sense that their parents do not make much of a difference in their lives. Mom and Dad are too preoccupied with their own problems and needs to provide any significant help to their kids. The result is a generation of teens who develop a fatalistic and resigned view of the world. As a result, kids try to make sense out of the world on their own. What else can they do? But underneath their "I can do it by myself" exterior is a broken inner world of disappointment, hurt, and betrayal.

Overworked parents have pushed these kids into a world they are not prepared to handle. The kids do the best they can, but we should not be surprised that many are not up to the task. For some kids, the sense that they must "parent" themselves is a constant source of anxiety and dread. For others, the fact that they have been set adrift by parental and familial authorities is a green light to all kinds of self-destructive behaviors.

Closeness Can Breed Conflict

Maybe one of the reasons many parents avoid parenting is because conflict between parents and kids is a daily part of family life. This conflict typically shows up in two ways:

- the spontaneous skirmishes that erupt over day-to-day matters, such as what clothes kids should wear, how much they should work on their homework, how much time they get at the computer, maintenance of their room, and issues of basic communication
- arguments over more significant or global issues, such as conflict over kids' driving habits, potential substance abuse, grades, dating, and friendships

Such conflicts are inevitable, but bubbling underneath the surface of these daily disagreements are important issues that parents need to understand.

What matters most in the lives of adolescents is how parents deal with conflict. Most kids rapidly get over the day-to-day battles they experience at home, especially if they feel close to their parents. But parents are not as resilient. Many parents allow even simple conflicts to push their emotional buttons and drive a wedge between them and their children.

Over time, kids who sense they are nothing more than a pain to their parents pull away from them. And kids who feel they cannot make a move without Mom or Dad laying down the law develop the sense that parents don't trust them.

The important thing parents need to remember about the daily conflicts that occur with their children is not to allow these conflicts to entrap them emotionally or divert them from their larger parenting goals. There will always be conflicts. The thing to remember

Parental Success

Susan Cosio

Before the days of iPods and the Internet, I grew up singing to the radio. I remember Bill Withers' hit song, "Lean on Me." He suggested that at some point, we all face pain and sorrow, but we have friends to turn to for support.

As a child and adolescent, the lyrics of the song resonated with my desire for interdependence and a sense of community. I liked the honest acknowledgment that we all need one another. But somewhere along the road to adulthood, I lost that sense of dependence. I became part of a generation that too often slaps on a smile and tries to hide our weak spots. We get caught up in externals and meeting expectations. We wear T-shirts that proudly assert, "Life is good." That "good life" includes achievement, independence, and success—even when it comes to family matters.

. As Chap Clark points out, our perceived "success" as parents is often reflected in the achievements of our kids. Great parents, it seems, have children who test well, perform well, and play (sports) well. Bumper stickers announce to the world that our children are honor students. Later we paste college logos on our windows so everyone knows which competitive schools our children attend. We even mail holiday letters that describe our kids' achievements, and then wish a Merry Christmas, almost as an afterthought.

The pressure to perform that permeates our culture breaks down rather than builds community by fueling competition. As my children entered their teenage years, I noticed that kids who were friends in elementary school had become competitors by junior high, vying for the same spot on the team or in the orchestra. Many teens today define their social standing—even their acceptance by their parents—on the basis of GPAs, SATs, and championships won. No wonder their self-esteem and sense of identity are so precarious.

Parents who are neighbors and friends can become isolated from one another because of feeling "competitive" along with the kids. "What classes is your son taking?" we ask. "What is your daughter doing after she graduates?" Even when we join school listserves (a kind of email group serving parents and teachers) to foster communica-

is to focus on the dynamics of the relationship rather than the particular issues at hand.

Far too often students describe their parents as "out of control," "always mad," or "totally upset." Kids respond by backing down to avoid conflict and they become relationally disengaged. Over time, these kids want to put more and more space between themselves and their parents.

---

tion, we use them to brag through our questions: "How many AP classes can my gifted child take in ninth grade?"

We seldom share our struggles, because we don't want to admit that our families and our kids (and therefore our parenting skills) are not as "perfect" as we think people expect them to be. This leaves us feeling as isolated and abandoned as our teenagers, just when we need one another the most.

I finished reading *Hurt* at 2:00 a.m., just a few weeks after its release in 2005. As a parent of three teenagers, it resonated deeply within my heart, and I knew immediately that Chap had a message my university town needed to hear. So I organized a community event at which Chap spoke.

More than four hundred parents, teachers, principals, counselors, youth leaders, and physicians came together to focus on our *shared* concern about today's teens. We learned about the needs of our youth and our need to work together. People all over town and in our schools—even people who didn't attend the event—were reading the book and recommending it to one another.

Chap's research and writing continue to have an impact. That initial event spawned a parent support group through which we continued an honest dialogue. One member of the group started a parent blog so parents could openly (albeit anonymously) express concerns about their kids. Several of us initiated parenting education events in our schools to address issues such as depression and teen drug use, instead of the predictable "How to Get into a Competitive College" workshops we had previously attended.

These events and follow-up groups have led to a greater openness in my own life, and in the lives of many other parents. We have strengthened our community and our relationships with our youth, as we have come together to navigate the sometimes messy, sometimes turbulent, but ultimately life-giving waters of parenting teens.

Susan Cosio is a hospital chaplain, providing family-centered care to children and adolescents. She and her husband Gib are imperfect parents of a daughter and two sons. They live in Davis, California.

De-fragmenting the Church Family

Bill MacPhee

Are we in student ministries contributing to the fragmentation of families? Through our apparent programmatic success we have created two churches: one for adults and one for kids. Our adults and students love their churches, but they rarely intersect. Our concern increases as we see so few of our graduating students continuing their connection to our church, or any church. Time-starved, consumer-savvy parents are appreciative of what our youth ministry offers, but also demand the "product" deliver the spiritual goods their schedule can't.

We're forcing ourselves to wrestle through theological implications of "church as family" metaphors in the Bible, with its emphasis on diversity and multiple generations all in one community. Is the church merely a collection of "niche" programs targeting various demographics, or does the biblical canvas detail something more organic, relational, and interconnected?

One practical step we are taking to address family fragmentation in our environment is to change how we accomplish the task of discipleship through our student ministries programming. Though we have hosted a large-group gathering of high school students on Sunday mornings for several decades, we have decided to shift these program resources and combine them with our Wednesday night small groups. Now we meet midweek for an extended time for large-group teaching and singing and then move into small groups of seven to ten students with an adult leader.

In moving these resources to midweek, we have intentionally freed up and framed the weekend as the time for the church family to worship together. Rather than piling out of cars, or even arriving in separate vehicles, and going in five different directions for individual programs, we plan a more relaxed pace where many generations get to

Kids Still Want Parents

This may seem to contradict what I just said, but it's true—kids want time with their parents. When I ask kids if they would like to have a closer relationship with their parents, most will fidget or stammer for a while before saying, "Yes, I guess I would like to be closer, but . . ."

It's what comes after the *but* that parents need to pay attention to:

- "but they are always on my back."

100

know and support one another. Welcoming adolescents into the core church life and relationships is more than just sitting in a worship service together, but the paradigm change gives space for us to be with and for one another, no matter our age.

The shift has forced significant reflections with challenging implications. Why would we give up a successful program that students and parents loved and replace it with kids moving back into the adult worship services? What student would choose attendance at an adult meeting over one packed with peers? Church leadership has had to admit we had taken over from parents the responsibility of spiritual nurture and have not provided helpful resources for equipping parents to lead their own kids. In more honest moments, some parents frankly don't like worship services that now include teenagers as legitimate participants. It was more comfortable before when the younger, more boisterous, fidgety crowd was essentially sequestered in the "youth room."

Fragmentation within families, hectic schedules, and the way we separated students from the center of our church demanded a practical response. We didn't want any young person to be left to navigate the rapids alone. Nor did we consider it an option to tell parents they were on their own. As a church family we now encourage parents to be proactive and invite other caring adults into the life of their family to invest in their children—not just on Sunday morning but every day.

Bill MacPhee, Associate Pastor of Family Ministries at Rolling Hills Covenant Church in Rolling Hills Estates, California (www.rollinghillscovenant.com, www.canvascommunity.net), has worked with students and families for thirty years. He received his doctor of ministry in Youth and Family Ministries at Fuller Theological Seminary. He has been married to Cynthia for twenty-three years and has two children. He loves to surf, bike, and read.

Bill is the President of ParenTeen (www.ParenTeen.com), an organization that delivers the research and input from *Hurt* and *Disconnected* to churches, organizations, and communities through seminars and materials.

- "but they don't know how to listen to me."
- "but they don't know how to be a friend."

Kids don't like conflict any more than parents do, but unless they view the family relationship as irreparably fractured, typically they tell me they still want to be closer to their parents. These answers affirm the results of a 2000 White House study that found "teens rated 'not having enough time together with their parents as one of their top problems.'"

Parenting Proactively

Over the last quarter century, we've all heard a lot of heated culture war rhetoric about the family. One of the words I've heard too much is *culture*, which has become a handy guilty party that people can blame for our kids' problems. Some people seem to say: "Hey, it's our 'culture' that's messing up our kids, not us!"

You can't change culture by yourself, but you can change the culture of your family. Here's how.

Show Up

The most important thing parents can do is be involved in the lives of their kids. I know—young people can often seem like an alien life form that is unbelievably confusing and complex. At the same time, parents who lovingly seek to understand their kids in the midst of the profound biological, psychological, and social transformations they are going through will be better positioned to

Putting into Practice

Involving Parents in Youth Ministry, Even if They Aren't the Cleavers

David Fraze

After following Chap's work, debating it with my students, and testing his conclusions in my area schools, churches, and speaking events, I have changed the way I speak of "family."

I was raised in a *Leave It to Beaver*–type family, at least in some ways. As a result I have been guilty of unknowingly using language that alienates those whose family arrangement is anything but traditional.

For example, hosting a Dad and Daughter Banquet can be a great ministry tool, but what if your "dad" is your grandfather? (This is becoming a rather common occurrence.) The situation can be more than awkward for the daughter and "dad." The solution may be as simple as expanding the definition of "dad" to include all male guardians and communicating that understanding when the event is offered. Expanding the definition of family goes a long way in helping everyone feel welcome in the faith community.

The way I involve parents in my youth ministry has also changed. I have always used parents and other caring adults in youth ministry. I have even encouraged them to provide an anchor of stability that can actually help kids navigate these turbulent waters.

Some of us have made the mistake of thinking of adolescence as the "teen years." But, as I pointed out earlier, due to changes in biology and society, adolescence now lasts up to fifteen years or more. Parents need to see their parental role as a marathon, not a sprint. And they need to be present in their kids' lives so they can build solid relationships of affection and trust that will stand the test of time.

Bend but Don't Break

Teens need room and flexibility so they can develop their own personalities and approaches for succeeding in life. Or in social science lingo, they need the autonomy to create their own identity and internal locus of control.

If teens feel their parents want to prevent this from happening, they will seek separation and isolation. But as we have seen, most kids would like their parents to be involved in their lives.

view their roles as sponsors, hosts, teachers, van drivers, or cooks as ministry. Still, I think the parents serving with me have had the idea that they were somewhat secondary players and support staff instead of key members of the ministry. Most of the adults had entered youth ministry service when their kids got into the program and quickly left when their kids graduated. Don't get me wrong; I really appreciated the service of these parents and any time they were able to give the ministry, but now, after *Hurt*, I view the role of parents with even more importance. I still ask parents to help with activities—this will never change—but I challenge them to view the informal times spent with teenagers with greater care and awareness. The results are encouraging. Parents are deepening relationships with their own kids, and kids from "broken" homes are finding caring adults to whom they can look for support.

David Fraze, with a doctor of ministry, serves as Director of Student Ministries at Richland Hills Church of Christ in North Richland Hills, Texas (www.247-rhcc.org). He is a key presenter with ParenTeen ministries (www.parenteen.com). He serves as adjunct professor of youth and family ministry at Lubbock Christian University; has been the host of a local TV segment, "The Teenage Tightrope" (www.theteenagetightrope.com); and has written articles for youthspecialties.com and *ENGAGE*, the quarterly journal of The Center for Parent/Youth Understanding.

Ministers to the Whole Family, Not Just Their Adolescents

Jeff Mattesich

Chap's section on the family in his book *Hurt* helped us assess what our ministry was doing to come alongside parents. We had fallen into the trap of niche ministry to students without realizing the need for and focusing on ministry to the entire family, especially parents. In an attempt to apply the research, we have taken the following steps.

First, we have successfully asked the church to have our college ministry move under the banner of student ministries. We feel that if we can help the church and our families see the lengthening of adolescence into college (and beyond), then any ministry to parents can be extended beyond the high school years of their child's life. When trying to deal with their children's problems, many parents of college students felt alone and lost at the church because of the assumption that their children are now "adults," at least at church.

We have poised ourselves very differently in relationship to families than in the past. We are constantly reminding parents that we exist to come alongside the entire family and that we are not just a ministry to students. We send out a monthly e-newsletter in which we include links to articles and books that can help parents, and more of our office time is spent in dialogue with them. We have seen a great increase in the number of families with whom we are in relationship and a great increase in families who are receptive to our ministry's helping and supporting them. It has very much changed the focus of what our ministry is about.

Jeff Mattesich is Associate Pastor of Children and Students at Lake Avenue Church in Pasadena, California.

Parents must provide a safe, warm environment for their teens while simultaneously maintaining a stable force of authority and control. Parents must seek to understand their children but must also provide flexible and reasonable boundaries that will allow them the opportunity to change and grow, relate to others, and make choices that matter.

Developing appropriate boundaries and adapting them to new needs as they emerge is a delicate dance. It requires a combination of understanding and energy. But you can do it if you try.

Accepting the Challenge

In many ways the task of parenting has never been more difficult. There are few rules to guide the process, which requires tedious negotiation and constantly shifting expectations. Unfortunately, many parents have given up. Through their inaction they have allowed pop culture, peers, and other forces to assume the parenting duties they have abdicated.

But when parents recognize what their children need and commit to providing the time and energy required of them, they have the opportunity to help their kids become strong, healthy, interdependent adults. The fruit of this carefully cultivated relationship is a lifelong friendship that you will enjoy for decades to come.

More Resources for Parents and Others Who Care for Kids

The issues we've explored in this chapter are explored more fully in two recommended resources created by Chap Clark.

1. *Disconnected: Parenting Teens in a MySpace World* is Chap and Dee Clark's 2007 book exploring many of the challenges and joys of raising teens today. The book is available at bookstores, online outlets, and from ParenTeen.

2. ParenTeen is the organization Chap created to make the research and insights from *Hurt* and *Disconnected* available to churches, organizations, and communities through seminars and materials.

   COMMUNITY PARENTEEN™ SEMINARS are for any adults who care for kids and are typically sponsored by social, civic, or church-based groups.

   CHURCH-BASED PARENTEEN™ SEMINARS present much of the same material but do so in a way that accents biblical principles of parenting and discipleship.

   The seminars are presented by Duffy Robbins, Marti Burger, Chuck Neder, David Fraze, and other youth leaders.

   For more information, visit www.parenteen.com.

7

good sports

One recent Saturday I attended a peewee football game. One of the players was the son of a close friend. The players were seven to nine years old, and most of them could barely hold their heads up when they ran, most likely due to the weight of the helmets they wore. They dressed like miniature pros, right down to the neck rolls and taped fingers. But most of them wandered, yelled, pouted, and ran like little children.

The sidelines were packed with parents, either videotaping or chewing their nails. Most were yelling. And indeed, the end was a nail-biter. "Our" team needed to somehow take the ball away from the other team if they were to get one last chance to score.

The man next to me, camera in hand, nearly lost his hat as he screamed at his son, "If you don't strip the ball, you're walking home!"

As I worked on this book, I seldom encountered such a clear and concise expression of the abandonment that plagues today's young people. But what a shock it was to hear this from a dad who should have been encouraging and rooting for his son!

My wife, a relationally sensitive but nonetheless experienced football mom, and I glanced at each other, not believing what we had just heard. Sure, we had been passionate sideline parents ourselves and had seen our share of over-the-top parental enthusiasm. How this man behaved, however, stunned us completely. His venom was so pointed, his threat so real, that we both actually feared for the boy were he to miss the play.

Sure enough, no one was able to strip the ball, and the team we were rooting for lost another game. The son cried as he approached his father, who remained oblivious to his son's emotional needs. "I guess you can't win 'em all," he barked. "Let's get the hell out of here!"

Winners and Losers

Stories like this one hint at what every high school student athlete has experienced on some level. The pressure is intense to compete, to excel, to perform, and to remain in the game.

But over time student athletes begin to see that there is a division between the first-team players and everyone else. By the time an athlete gets to high school, his or her chance to participate in team sport has already been all but settled. Sure, an outsider could catch the eye of a coach and be catapulted above others to active participation. But in most high school sports, the main players are set even before the season begins. The ones who are safely nestled into the security of a starting spot are called jocks, and most of them wear the badge proudly.

There are, of course, many positive aspects to high school sports, and they have been well documented. A recent report from the American Psychological Association's *Healthy Adolescents Project* found that sports allow adolescents to get exercise, make friends, learn about teamwork, and build character. They can also be, for many, fun.

But few students participate in these activities for exercise or friendship. For the most part, by the time athletes get to high school, the level of expectation and the pressure to perform make their participation an all-consuming commitment. For many athletes, even the nice and concerned coaches can be hardheaded, demanding, and, while seemingly committed to what's best for each student, ultimately are more concerned with what's best for the team.

Kids Dabbling in Doping

With the Tour de France now off and peddling under a cloud of doping allegations, it's interesting to note that even prepubescent children are experimenting with performance enhancing drugs.

The study of French sixth graders found that more than 1 percent were dabbling in doping. Four years later—when they would be the equivalent to sophomores in high school—3 percent were using. Half the children who admitted to using said they had won at least one sporting event as a result.

There are many reasons adolescents do not participate in sports: cost, lack of transportation, time commitment, and so on. What was not on the list is what I believe to be the most important reason of all. There are not enough opportunities for "average" student athletes to compete.

Even if there were more chances for participation, I am convinced that few of these average players would enlist, mostly because they have been told since before junior high that they don't have what it takes to be an athlete. This attitude creates inside the developing identity of an early adolescent a defining stereotype that most have a hard time shaking. Trying to convince a late-blooming tenth grader to try out for basketball is to ask him to risk a great deal, especially if he was derided as a child or early adolescent. One more rejection, especially for the fragile midadolescent, may be one too many to risk.

Researchers Merrill Melnick, Kathleen Miller, and Donald Sabo found that high school sports teach kids a mixed bag of lessons:

> Coaches, athletic administrators, the mass media, and the general public often assert that interscholastic athletic participation helps teenagers develop healthy habits while steering them away from tobacco, alcohol, drugs, dangerous dietary practices, physical inactivity, and other detrimental behaviors. . . .

On the other hand, some sport critics focus on a variety of negative health-related behaviors they believe are associated with athletic participation such as binge drinking; drug use; on- and off-the-field aggression; . . . eating disorders, amenorrhea, and osteoporosis; actions that result in unintentional injury and death, such as irresponsible automobile, motorcycle, and bicycle use; and unprotected sex.

In my experience, adults' opinions about their children were greatly influenced according to whether their children were "slow" or "gifted" with regard to sports. Parents of nonathletes had to create an explanation for the crushing disappointment of exclusion and often saw sports in a negative light.

Most schools are home to many more non-all-stars than all-stars, but that doesn't mean there is room for all to play. That's because by the time second-stringers enter high school, the die has been cast, and the athletic roles they will play throughout their high school years have already been settled.

Youth Culture Update

Stronger, Faster, Younger

Just a game? C'mon. Children and their parents are taking their athletics pretty seriously these days, and a host of sports performance companies are catering to these jocks in the making.

Velocity, one such sports performance training company, says more than forty-seven thousand children participated in their programs nationwide in 2006—four times the company's enrollment just two years earlier. Most participating children are between the ages of twelve and fifteen, but some children begin as early as eight. For some uncoordinated children, the programs amount to remedial phys ed classes. But many are talented athletes already eying potential college scholarships.

"You can't get by with sitting around anymore," said eighteen-year-old Jordy Christian, a hockey player. "Once you settle into a sport, you make it your life."

In *The Hurried Child,* sociologist and child development guru David Elkind quotes sportswriter John Underwood, who took on the Little Leagues more than two decades ago in *Sports Illustrated.* Here's what Underwood said then: "To visit on small heads the pressure to win, the pressure to be 'just like mean Joe Green' is indecent. To dress children up like pros in costly outfits is ridiculous. In so doing, we take away many of the qualities that competitive sports are designed to give to the growing process."

More recently *Sports Illustrated* writer Alexander Wolff gave this mixed assessment of "The High School Athlete":

> The numbers—and what do sports train us to trust more than numbers?—tell us that high school athletics have never been healthier. Roughly four million boys and three million girls, more than ever before, participate in one or more of some 50 athletic endeavors before kiting off to the rest of their lives. . . . The win-at-all-costs coaches and preprofessional priorities commonplace in college sports have seeped into grades 12, 11, 10 and below. . . . As coaches demand year-round proof of dedication, kids spend a greater and greater proportion of time practicing rather than playing, and many state high school federations, which once enforced strict rules on summer activities, throw up their hands, sometimes eliminating those rules altogether.

Superstars and Nobodies

I sat down with three groups to figure out how kids feel about the way we do sports today. First, I met with a group that consisted of preadolescent athletes. There were three boys who played organized baseball and three girls who played competitive soccer, all between ages eight and ten. Most were from relatively affluent, intact families in which there was a great deal of emotional support. They all considered themselves "good" to "pretty good" at sports.

They were at the highest level in their respective sports and they did not feel it was wrong for them to get to go to special tournaments, get more playing time than other kids, and be separated from the "not-so-good athletes" in how they were treated by coaches, parents, and their teammates. Not only did they feel fine about

111

this performance segregation but they felt it was "more fair" than letting poorer athletes take playing time away from them. Every one of these children believed that the good should get to play, and those who weren't good should have to wait until they (the better athletes) were tired. "If we're better than they are, then why should we suffer?" one child said.

My second group consisted of seniors in high school athletics: three male baseball players and three female soccer players, who had always been starters. While they acknowledged that other children's feelings could possibly get hurt if they were not given much playing time, they seemed to deflect any understanding of how it must feel for those kids. As much as they tried to feign concern for those who were not born with athletic skill and talent, they had little compassion for the nonathletic students.

The third group I met with consisted of nonathletic seniors. As much as the first group was marked by entitlement and the second by defensiveness, the third was marked by hurt and even resentment. These seniors, who had been told at a fairly young age that they did not have the ability to participate in sports, left me sad and a bit angry.

The stories varied, from a boy who quit sports because his third grade soccer coach told him his play was costing the team games, to a girl who lost her best friends in fifth grade when she was cut from a competitive soccer team (the pain was as fresh as if it had happened the day before). Most of these students hated jocks and everything related to sports.

I walked away from these conversations wondering how our culture had gotten to this unhappy point. In our competitive and performance-driven world, by the time children are in the fourth or fifth grade, they're told whether they "have it" or they don't. For a variety of reasons, this message is not in and of itself enough to cause lasting damage to an adolescent. Some kids who are told they don't have it become firmly committed to showing a coach, friend, or parent how wrong they are.

Yet we have a long way to go in understanding how our intensity concerning sports has impacted our young, especially those who have been excluded from participation and denied a sense of personal worth because they developed late, were not able to

112

contribute, or simply got in the way of a coach's, a parent's, or even a teammate's drive to excel.

Every adult was reared on the notion that sports build character in children. But in light of what I have seen, little true character is being built. In fact I have observed just the opposite. True character is built when one is rewarded for hard work, when one is willing to sacrifice for a friend or teammate, when one experiences the instilled value that proclaims the love of sport and not the lust for competition.

The competitive world of student sports is perhaps the most obvious arena in which abandonment has made its mark on the adolescent psyche. We still use the rhetoric that youth sports build character, yet, in reality, often what we have taught our children builds nothing other than arrogance, self-centeredness, and a performance ethic that is destructive to healthy, communally connected development.

Winners or Losers

In some schools and among some students, athletes enjoy the same privileged position they did when their parents went to school. What's changed is this: jocks can no longer claim priority on the highest rungs of the school status ladder. Instead, the historically definable and clearly observable social ladder is being dismantled in favor of a more complex web of social influence.

In the school where I conducted this study, athletics still mean a great deal, but even at this school, jocks were no more esteemed than any other group, including the band. Students no longer put up with the stereotype that athletes rule the school, and perhaps in a subconscious attempt to get back at the childhood athletic systems that hurt them, many nonathletes disdain jocks.

Still, the stigma that accompanies inferior sports performance can hurt. And it is not just *some* students who have suffered at the hands of a culture of abandonment when it comes to the decay of play and fun. All have suffered for our culture's crazy approach to athletics.

Let's look at three athletes whom I had the opportunity to study in depth. Craig is a star water polo player. Carrie is a dancer on

The Cost of Competitive Sports

Bill Duppenthaler

The chapter on sports in *Hurt* hit very close to home for me. I was a year-round competitive swimmer in high school who felt compelled to choose between pursuing my faith through a Young Life club or continuing to pursue competitive swimming. In the end, I chose to give up swimming. It was a difficult choice because it meant essentially changing my whole social structure at the time as well. The great thing was, after that I was really able to get much more involved with Young Life and my church, because I was not always so tired from all year long "two-a-days."

As parents, Jody and I have bucked the tide of popular opinion that says good parents enroll their kids in all the select sports programs they can handle. Our kids participated in a variety of sports programs, but not the elite programs, before they realized that if they were not willing to totally give everything they have to one sport, most likely they would not have a chance of making the team at the high school. Should I have pushed them harder? Did I let them down?

I have had the opportunity to coach many sports over the years at all levels. To me it has been frustrating to see sports become such an all-consuming thing for so many kids, when all they really wanted to do was just to have fun.

A recent experience highlighted for me the sad state of affairs that we're in today with competitive sports. A high school student who had agreed to referee a game I was coaching told me he couldn't do so after all. The coach of the team he played on had called an unscheduled practice. I convinced the student to honor his commitment; then I talked to the coach and explained that the student had made a prior

what is called the varsity Song Squad. Grant is a second-string football player.

Craig

Craig, the water polo player, is a naturally gifted player, but he is also a leader in a sport that is considered second tier (compared to football, basketball, or baseball), and he therefore feels the need to convince people that water polo players are "the best athletes in the school." This need to prove himself has become a major element of his personality and relationships. He can no longer play

commitment to ref our game. The coach turned a deaf ear to me and later penalized the student for showing insufficient commitment to his team.

Commitment and leadership are great attributes to learn and there are opportunities to learn other life lessons from participation in sports as well—things like the fact that hard work pays off, the value of teamwork and sacrifice, learning how to deal with successes or failures, seeing the results of goal setting and determination, and the list goes on and on. For so many kids, however, what I see happening instead is they get turned off to sports altogether because either they are told they are not good enough or they choose not to make the all-out, year-round sacrifice to be on the team. If they do end up participating in high school sports, it becomes the all-consuming focus of their lives.

In an advanced version of what it was like for me on the swim team in high school, today's high school athletes have a difficult if not impossible time being involved with something like Young Life or a church youth group during sport season. Even during the off-season, there are so many expectations placed on them (club teams; off-season weightlifting, conditioning, and training programs; specialty camps and off-season leagues) that they have a tough time going to youth group camps, weekend retreats, or even small-group Bible studies.

It is sad to me when kids are not allowed (by their parents or the coach) to go to summer camp because they will miss a week of summer conditioning for a fall sport.

Bill Duppenthaler has been working with kids in Young Life for more than thirty years. Having been immersed in the youth culture since 1976, Bill has devoted his professional life to understanding, connecting to, and communicating with teenagers. As a Senior Area Director with Young Life, currently serving in Gig Harbor, Washington, Bill works closely with a team of volunteer leaders in Young Life, along with the local public schools, churches, and parachurch organizations, to maximize effective outreach. Bill and his wife, Jody, have impacted thousands of kids and are raising three high schoolers of their own.

for fun and sport. He must make sure that others know that he, as a water polo player, matters.

Carrie

Carrie has always loved to dance. As a little girl, trying out new moves for her parents, putting on a fancy dress for the Christmas recital, and freely floating around a room with giggling friends made the pain of learning how to stand on her toes worthwhile. But when she started fourth grade, dance was no longer a joyous adventure of free expression. It had shifted to a physically grueling gauntlet every weekday as she prepared for the next competition. By fifteen the pressure from the driven coach, the early morning practices, the continual (misguided and unnecessary) fight with her weight, and the daily pressure not to mess up and hurt the team had taken its toll. She quit the team after one year on varsity. She had lost her love of dance while becoming a dancer.

Grant

Grant was never quite good enough, or so the head varsity coach told him, to play "at this level." He had played football since he was ten, had even started for most of his sophomore season. But once he got to varsity, the head coach made it clear that he was barely welcome. He would be on the team but he should not expect to play.

As much as Grant saw himself as a football player, and his cluster and others on the team treated him as an equal, the coach never came around. Grant received an award at the banquet, but the head coach made it clear that he had not contributed. When I asked the other guys about Grant and the coach, the response was predictable: "The coach is a jerk. Grant should have started, at least a few games. He was a leader on the team." Apparently the coach was too concerned about being in charge to care about whom he hurt in the process. Grant's saving grace was his cluster. His friends showed compassion, loyalty, and concern.

No Longer Fun

Three students, three sports, three experiences; in their own ways, these students allowed me to see how coaches and parents have added a layer of performance anxiety to their love of sport. The stories are unique, as are the circumstances, but the backdrop for the struggles they face comes from the same source—they are the casualties of systemic abandonment by those charged with their care. As they explained to me, sports (including dance) are no longer about fun, exercise, experience, and play. They are about competition, winning, and defeating an opponent. Sports are no longer child's play; they are a grown-up, dog-eat-dog reality.

What Have We All Lost?

During this study, I became more convinced of how insidious and self-serving youth and high school competitive activities have become. These activities are no longer for or about the students; they are for and about the adults in charge. The deification of competitive prominence and the defeat of one's "enemies" have choked much of the life out of the human desire to play for play's sake and even to compete with class and honor.

Of course there are exceptions to this, as there are to nearly everything else I have said in this book. I got to know many of the coaches at the school where I taught, and as individuals, they are a top-notch lot. The competitive academic athletic environment in which they operate, however, is focused on competitive excellence, and it's taking its toll on our young. A sensitive, savvy coach in an overly competitive system may be able to ensure that the sport or the season does as little developmental damage as possible, but the pressure of winning and performing is a large force indeed.

As with every aspect of the consequences of abandonment, the most potent tool we have in helping adolescents overcome the damage caused by the negative aspects of sports is to help them see that, in the final analysis, competition doesn't matter. We've been giving lip service to this message for decades—"It's all about trying your best, kids. It's not winning that counts; it's how you play the game"—but our rhetoric has not lined up with our behavior.

When the father of the football team's kicker screamed at his son in front of hundreds of parents and students after he missed an extra point, the message of "doing your best" became merely a convenient and hollow post-game speech coaches use to try to motivate athletes following a loss. Shame on that father! And shame on us for allowing a destructive system to continue in the name of sport.

It used to be fun to play sports, but for far too many of the students I talked to, their involvement ceased to be fun a long time ago. I cannot think of any other area of life in which we as a society have abandoned our young more thoroughly. From the time they hear "Play ball!" they know that they had better come through and perform, even if they are only playing for fun.

117

8

sexual but not satisfied

We live in a sexually saturated and sexually confused culture. Adolescents grow up in a society that is simultaneously obsessed and repressed, pornographic and puritanical. Other cultures don't know what to make of us and our sexuality. Many people around the world know us only by our TV shows and movies, which reduce sexuality to one juvenile, narcissistic escapade after another. People in Europe and much of South America see Americans as sexually repressive and arrogantly naïve. In much of Asia, the Middle East, and Africa, Americans are seen as decadents who are bent on destroying centuries-old cultural, religious, and familial traditions.

I wanted to discover how today's teens view sex and sexuality. And while some of what I found surprised or even shocked me, one thing did not. The main thing I saw was that today's adolescents are not as saturated with sex as they are drowning in loneliness. The abandonment that we have explored in earlier chapters reveals itself in the sexual anxiety of today's teens.

I thought the high school boys and girls I got to know would easily and constantly be swept up in a world of sexual lust and wild, irresponsible relational dalliances. I was surprised to realize

119

A Trojan Horse?

The Centers for Disease Control released a shocking study March 10, 2008. The study claimed one-fourth of all American girls between the ages of fourteen and nineteen have at least one sexually transmitted disease (STD).

Who responded to this study? Church leaders? Youth or family ministry folks? Educators? Lawmakers or politicians? Nope.

Instead it was Trojan, the condom company, which ran a full-page ad in *USA Today* the following week, saying: "American teens are in a health crisis, and nothing will change unless we act." The ad ended with the following website: www. trojancondoms/act.

that for most midadolescents the issue of sex has lost its mystique and has become almost commonplace.

Today's teens have been conditioned to expect so much from sex and simultaneously tainted by its overexposure and emptiness that they have become jaded in their attitudes. "Sex is a game," one student told me, "a toy, nothing more." As I was to find out, it is also more than that. Sex serves as a temporary salve for the pain and loneliness today's adolescents feel.

Slumber Party Bingo

Let me offer a story that happened in my own town while I was working on this book. The incident took place during a seventh-grade-girls sleepover when the host girl's parents were home, and it illustrates the dark, new world where midadolescents live. During the course of the evening, a seventh-grade boy came over to the house and, after some small talk with the mother hosting the event, was sent up to the host girl's bedroom. The parents knew the boy, so they did not think twice about letting him visit the girls for a few minutes.

Of the six girls attending the party, five were from intact families with caring, upper-middle-class parents. The sixth girl lived with her mother and a supportive, involved stepfather. Four of the girls and their families were self-described Christians and were actively involved in faith communities. The girls were popular with peers, involved with extracurricular activities, and were close to their mothers and fathers. In short, you could not comb a junior high in America and find a better sample of exemplary adolescents.

The boy lived with a supportive single mother and two younger siblings. He had no previous romantic experience, and his relationships with girls had always been as friends. He had come over simply because he lived nearby, was bored, and was friends with these girls. Apparently he had no preconceived ulterior motives.

After this boy had been in the room for thirty minutes or so, the mother decided to check on the girls. When she heard some giggling coming from the room, she decided to investigate. When she opened the door to the bedroom unannounced, she was shocked by what she saw.

The six girls were on their knees in a line with the boy standing in front of them with his pants down. The girls were taking turns performing oral sex on the boy.

The boy was obviously embarrassed but seemed more scared that he had been busted. He pulled up his pants and hurried out of the house.

The girls were embarrassed, too, and worried about what punishment they would receive.

But aside from the threatened punishment, they didn't really feel that they had done anything wrong. In fact some felt that if a wrong had been committed, it was the mother who had no right to enter the room without knocking.

In Search of Morality

As I talked to groups of teens about sexuality, I asked them what they thought about this episode. The responses from both males and females ranged from mild amazement to resigned acknowledgment that, while not exactly appropriate, the event was not surprising. But I never saw any moral outrage among the kids. Some girls wondered how the girls at the slumber party could be so "stupid," but for the most part, both boys and girls seemed to recognize that this is a normal experience in their world, the kind of thing that happens when adolescents follow through on their impulses.

"Was this wrong?" was my standard query.

"I don't know about wrong exactly, but it wasn't very smart," one girl in a group told me. Many teens agreed with her.

"These kids were experimenting," said an eighteen-year-old senior girl. "They didn't really know what they were doing. They were just trying to have fun. They probably saw it in a movie and figured it was kind of cool. But they were idiots for not locking the door!"

I was astounded that this episode was considered "normal" by these students.

When I asked if it would have been more shocking if sixteen-year-olds had done this, I was told, "It would have happened only

Sex Education

Girls who have sex at a young age are more likely to feel depressed, according to a recent study, than older girls. But there are caveats.

According to the study, girls who were in a long-term relationship that involved sex showed no greater inclination to feel blue than those who were not having sex. And, while girls who had sex as part of a failed short-term relationship were markedly more apt to feel depressed, the study found they weren't any more down than girls who had just broken up and hadn't had sex.

Ann Meier, a professor at the University of Minnesota and the study's author, believes that age isn't a huge factor in the link between depression and sex, but societal norms—the average age when girls become sexually active. Just what age that is varies from culture to culture, from 15.2 years for African Americans to 17.5 years for Americans of Asian descent.

Abstinence Up—Abstinence Education Down

Teens these days are more likely to remain virgins longer and, if they do have sex, they're more likely to use contraception. Despite this, abstinence education in many public school systems is under attack.

Eleven states have rejected abstinence education programs this year, while three others recently passed laws that could eliminate or cripple such programs already in play. This year, the United States Senate opted to cut funding for abstinence education for the first time since 2001.

The problem is that, while teens seem to be staying abstinent longer, abstinence education doesn't seem to make a whit's worth of difference. In fact, teens who had abstinence education had sex at a slightly higher rate than those who hadn't had abstinence education at all.

with girls who were so drunk that they didn't know or care or girls who were just stupid."

Would a guy do it, I asked? "Absolutely!" they said. "Any guy. Every guy!"

What's the Big Deal?

There are no longer any rules regarding sexuality in mainstream society, especially for adolescents. The fact that a group of eleven-year-olds can so easily participate in such sexual antics reveals that we are far removed from Victorian sexual morality. By the time a typical child reaches ten or eleven years of age, he or she has seen—on television and in movies—and heard about not only sexual intercourse but also oral sex, "threesomes," masturbation, anal sex, rape, bestiality, and many other forms of sexual expres-

123

Same-Sex Education

Montgomery County, Maryland, is now offering lessons on homosexuality to eighth, ninth, and tenth grade students in its public health education classes.

The lessons consist of two forty-five-minute, heavily scripted classes per grade that include instructions on how to put on a condom. Supporters say the classes are done with an eye toward tolerance and cultural literacy. Critics believe the county's schools are going too far.

National public opinion on the matter is mixed. According to a 2004 Kaiser Family Foundation survey, about three-quarters of parents of high schoolers and half of parents of middle schoolers say that it's appropriate for schools to teach students about homosexuality. Most, however, say that teaching should be done without saying whether being gay is right or wrong. Only 8 percent of high school parents and 4 percent of middle school parents feel that schools should say that homosexuality is "morally acceptable."

sion and experimentation. It has been decades since the "innocent" young were shielded from these behaviors.

But our children and early adolescents are subjected to this daily barrage of sexual expression and innuendo without understanding how relational and psychosocial dynamics intersect with sexual activity. As I talked to the kids during my study, sexual joking and sexual language were common and even intrusive. Not a week went by that I was not somehow shocked by the explicit nature of sexuality on the campus. Here's a sampling of what I encountered in just one week:

- A group of girls was judging a guy's backside. Pleased with the attention, he erotically posed for the judges.

124

- A student dropped a note that was filled with a sexually explicit description of the adventures she planned with two male students.
- I walked in on a couple embracing and kissing. The boy's arm was under the girl's thong, which was exposed above her low-cut jeans.

Defining Virginity Down

While sex has become a pervasive aspect of adolescent life, some believe the rate at which adolescents engage in sexual intercourse has, paradoxically, gone down. Birth rates and abortion rates have decreased, at least according to some studies. And some students believe their sexual standards are high.

This is partly because adolescents tend to define sex as intercourse, or penile penetration in a vagina. Everything else, including oral sex or anal sex, is not considered sex—which means a great deal of adolescent sexual contact is written off by adolescents themselves through definition technicalities. Those who want to can claim virginity because they haven't gone "all the way," yet many have few qualms about engaging in scads of risqué behavior.

There seems to be little debate that, regardless of whether adolescents are engaging less often in intercourse, their rate of sexual activity has greatly increased, and it's now considered normal for even a casual dating relationship. Most who are not "sexually active" are nonetheless sexually intimate.

I met dozens of self-proclaimed virgins who regularly practiced many forms of sexual intimacy with multiple partners and who displayed no feelings of guilt or moral incongruity—even when they said they were committed to "staying pure." This behavior demonstrates that the very definition of sex has changed in fundamental ways.

But while adolescents may have redefined sex on their own terms, they have not been so lucky in escaping its sometimes-brutal emotional ramifications. During the study, I saw several instances where students became angry over sexual relationships gone awry. These outbursts ranged from the "cold shoulder" to near violent breakups after months or even years of sexual experimentation.

Talking the Birds and Bees with Teens—Continually

Kara Powell and Jim Hancock

In the midst of kids' loneliness and sexual experimentation, wouldn't it be nice to have a reasonable, direct, honest, genuine, hopeful conversation about sex? Wouldn't it be good for our kids to hear us speak of God's good gifts in glowing, optimistic terms? Wouldn't it be wonderful to talk about sex without fear or anger or pretense?

Sadly, the church seems to have lost her voice on the topic of sex, partly from confusion and fear and partly from screaming herself hoarse. Those of us who aren't scared silent suffer a sort of cultural laryngitis: people see our lips moving but can't always make out what we're saying.

We've learned from experience that kids are open to talking about sex *with adults they trust*. But that conversation can't happen in just one sitting. Nor can it be done in one youth group talk about sex (no matter how great that talk is) or even an annual series on love, sex, and dating. That's because in the real world, kids encounter sexual information and experiences in a process that stretches over decades. Most of that information and quite a bit of the experience is indirect. They read, listen, watch television and movies, hang out with friends and acquaintances. They watch their parents and other adults. They watch their siblings and other peers. They experience sexual arousal (and it takes them by surprise).

Sexual jokes and flippancy sometimes covered feelings of genuine hurt and sadness.

Social science research is beginning to recognize that nonmarital sexual activity can have measurable negative consequences, and I saw this firsthand in the students I watched. They experienced heartache and betrayal in relation to their sexual encounters, and they expressed everything from rampant self-hate to unapologetic callousness.

Only the Lonely

The reasons for the decreasing age of intimate sexual activity are loneliness, the increased opportunity provided to kids who return to empty homes after school, and the pervasive sense of

From all these impressions, they construct a picture of what sex is—or appears to be. And out of that picture come their sexual attitudes, opinions, and actions. The picture is updated as they encounter new information and experiences and, even in adulthood, the picture is never complete as long as they're learning.

Contrast that with most teaching (as distinct from learning) about sex. Most of what kids get directly from adults is much less a process and much more a *confrontation*: "Here are the facts; remember them. These are the boundaries; don't cross them. This is the truth; believe it."

If we agree that experience is the best teacher (not the preferred teacher, perhaps, but the most effective), which of these seems likely to be more influential: *process* or *confrontation*? We think teaching about sex should be more a process than a confrontation because we think that's how people really learn.

"Well, we can't be always talking about love, sex, and dating," you say.

Why not? Once they reach puberty, kids are always talking about relationships with the other gender. They're exposed to films, books, magazines, games, websites, music, and television that constantly talk about sexuality. They live in a human context that is always, on one level or another, about sex. It's all part of the process. Except at church (and a few other adult-sensitive settings), where grown-ups typically *confront* instead of *process*. Come to think of it, the confrontation they usually get from adults becomes *part* of the larger process, whether it's a conscious choice or not. That's one reason kids don't believe it's safe to talk about sex when adults are in the room.

abandonment that I uncovered in every aspect of my research with kids.

Adolescent sexuality, and perhaps all human sexuality, is connected more to a desire for relational connection and a safe place than to a physical, albeit sometimes pleasurable, activity of the body. And many midadolescents are almost desperate in their loneliness. This is true for both girls and boys. They would prefer to experience sexual intimacy in the confines of a relationship, but it's not absolutely necessary for them. There is a genuine belief in the midadolescent world that sex with a relative stranger can be the route to happiness and fulfillment.

David Brooks of the *Weekly Standard* recounted his experience with college students who attempted to explain the difference between a "hook up" (casual sex with a relative stranger) and

An ancient Hebrew liturgy celebrates this *process* of leading kids into loving obedience to their invisible Creator. This liturgy, called *Shema*, says, in part:

Hear, O Israel: The LORD our God, the LORD is one. Love the LORD your God with all your heart and with all your soul and with all your strength. These commandments that I give you today are to be upon your hearts. Impress them on your children. Talk about them when you sit at home and when you walk along the road, when you lie down and when you get up. Tie them as symbols on your hands and bind them on your foreheads. Write them on the doorframes of your houses and on your gates.

Deuteronomy 6:4–9

That's process. That's the way the other guys—the people who don't share our beliefs or values—do it, whether they mean to or not. If we want to impress the next generation with biblically grounded values around sex, it's the way we should do it too.

Adapted with permission from Jim Hancock and Kara Powell, *Good Sex* (Grand Rapids: Zondervan, 2008).

Jim Hancock invested two decades as a church-based youth worker. Now he creates digital movies and learning designs for youth workers, parents, and adolescents, including, with Kara Powell, *Good Sex Curriculum*.

Kara Powell is Executive Director of the Fuller Youth Institute (www.fulleryouthinstitute.org) and is the author of a number of books, including *Deep Justice in a Broken World* (coauthored with Chap Clark), *Deep Ministry in a Shallow World* (coauthored with Chap Clark), and *Good Sex Curriculum* (coauthored with Jim Hancock).

the "hang out" (sex with someone after spending a bit of time together). He writes:

This is the point at which us fogies are supposed to lament the decline in courtship. Indeed, I was out drinking late one night with a group of students, and a woman to my left mentioned that she would never have a serious relationship with someone she wouldn't consider marrying. "That sounds traditional," I said to her. She responded, "I didn't say I wouldn't f—— anyone I wouldn't consider marrying."

Many students I encountered held loosely to the philosophy that sexual activity is generally better reserved for someone you love or at least are interested in, but that sentiment is not so strong that it precludes a random sexual encounter with a stranger given the opportunity.

Whatever Happened to Love and Romance?

Since conducting this study, I have had a difficult time watching television, going to movies, and driving by billboards on the freeway. I have been even more troubled by ads that use sexuality to market products to teens. I have long been aware of the sexual nature of our culture but now I see it in a new light and I fear for the impact our sexualized culture is having on the emotional and social development of our children and adolescents. I cannot help but lament the fact that we have lost any hope of maintaining sexual innocence and sanctity for the current generation.

We have undergone a massive shift over the last several decades. I can remember growing up with an appreciation for sex as a wonder and mystery. Sexual intercourse and the intersection of bodies was a symbol of the intersecting of minds, hearts, and spirits. But as I survey contemporary youth culture, such notions seem antiquated, if not extinct.

Will this generation be able to understand the sacred nature of such a physical act? As I listened to students talk about how they felt about love, romance, and sex, I had trouble finding any who could make the connection.

Other adults seem to share my concerns. Here's what writer Terri D. Fisher said in her review of the book *The Development of Romantic Relationships in Adolescence*:

> While the study of adolescent sexuality is of unquestionable importance, I am now amazed and saddened that so many of us have studied sexuality removed from its context, which is often, but certainly not always, a romantic relationship. It is ironic that scientists have neglected the study of adolescent romance since it is a topic of such great importance to so many teenagers.

Since the beginning of time, humanity has continually reminded itself that love, faithfulness, trust, and authentic intimate relationships are an essential part of what makes human life meaningful. The hope I carry is that the pendulum has swung as far as it can go in thinking about sex as a plaything and that it will be brought back to the center by generations who have seen how devastatingly empty frivolous sex can be.

129

For now, all we can do is remind the young of our culture that love matters, that people are not objects or playthings, and that our bodies and our hearts cannot be separated.

Adults will need to stay involved in this battle for a more balanced approach to sex. We will be bombarded by conflicting and discouraging messages but we will need to do whatever we can to help adolescents see the difference between sex as recreation and sex as a sacred aspect of human life and happiness.

9

our overstressed adolescents

So, does your life seem busy and hectic? Well, I have news for you. Many of today's midadolescents are busier than that. And they're not enjoying it any more than you are! The ever-mounting demands on their time and energies; the heightening expectations from coaches, bosses, and activity leaders; the proliferation of homework; and the accessibility of many communication options make the typical day in the life of a midadolescent a balancing act.

During my research, I saw that many were tired to the point of near exhaustion. They weren't lazy or bored; they were exhausted, the way I feel after staying up most of the night due to a delayed flight. That's because the typical teen averages five to six hours of sleep a night (while many child development experts argue that adolescents need eight to nine hours).

I was shocked by the stress I saw in the kids around me. I was not alone. "I have been working with kids for forty years," one social worker told me, "and today's kids are the most stressed out I have ever seen."

"They are on the edge, that's for sure," said another social worker who worked in the district where I was serving. "And the worst part is, they don't even know how stressed they are!"

131

The supervisor of a social services agency agreed. "They have no other framework, so they don't even know what stress is or looks like." The supervisor shared the following story.

"I was talking to a kid last week, a sharp junior—student government, involved as a leader in the YMCA Youth In Government program, a star volleyball player who looked like he would be a great student. But he told me he wouldn't be able to get into a four-year college because of his grades.

"He saw my expression and said, 'Man, I don't have time to do homework and I'm just too tired to stay awake in class. After volleyball, the Y, and Young Life, I have to gel and catch up with my friends. Just getting up in the morning is a miracle!'

"I tried to get him to step back and to see what's important, to get him to consider his future and make some priorities in his life. He just looked at me like I was his mom telling him to clean his room. All he said as he turned away was, 'You just don't get it, do you?'"

I had met with these social workers so we could talk about helping at-risk kids. But after sharing a long list of anecdotes about

Youth Culture Update

It's Not Easy Being Tween

Youth today are stressed. About 60 percent of teens and 50 percent of tweens say they're on edge, and reasons range from weight to grades to their relationship with their parents. Half of tweens say they're worried people will make fun of them; 19 percent fear getting beat up. For teens, weight's a big worry: 38 percent fret about it.

A good chunk of kids—70 percent—say they're getting enough attention at home. In fact 9 percent say they're spending too much time with their parents and they wish their moms and dads would just back off a little.

Girls are generally more stressed out than boys, with their biggest worry being grades. The only thing boys are more worried about than girls is going to war: nearly 25 percent of boys fear being shipped off to battle, compared to 10 percent of girls.

overstressed kids, no one had the energy to try to strategize something. The problem seemed to trivialize our feeble efforts to help. Like many of the adults in their lives, today's midadolescents seem to *want* to be incredibly busy. Or if they don't want this kind of lifestyle, they do not seem to know a different way of organizing their lives. And they are turned off by anyone's attempt to put limits on them or to suggest priorities and boundaries. Midadolescents live in the midst of the only reality they know. They are afraid of the unknown but are also exhausted in the present. The result of this commitment to busyness? Stress.

The consequences of the stress are real and powerful, yet few midadolescents see stress as a negative aspect of their lives. "It is what it is," one student told me when I asked why he was so tired. "I have to work, I have to be with my friends, I have to be up for practice, and I have to live my life. I'm doing okay, so don't hassle me—unless I snore in class."

The Reality of Their Lives

The busyness, fragmentation, and stress level adolescents experience are relatively new, and they are increasing. And today's kids are the victims of a culture that is out of control.

As David Elkind wrote in his classic study, *The Hurried Child*: "Today's child has become the unwilling, unintended victim of overwhelming stress—the stress born of rapid, bewildering social change and constantly rising expectations."

David Brooks of the *Weekly Standard* wrote about the stress felt by students at prestigious universities: "Their main lack is time. Students boast to each other about how little sleep they've gotten, and how long it's been since they had a chance to get back to their dorm room."

Brooks says students keep spinning because they know

> the system doesn't necessarily reward brains; it rewards energy. The ones who thrive are the ones who can keep going from one activity to another, from music, to science, to sports, to community service, to the library, and so on without rest. To get into a competitive school, you need a hyperactive thyroid as much as high intelligence.

▬ *Under Pressure* ▬

According to a study by the University of Michigan, almost two-thirds of high schoolers say they experience major stress at least once a day—and the reasons go far beyond the occasional pimple.

The key to destressing these kids, according to experts, is getting them to shift out of high gear once in a while. Parents need to make sure they're not overscheduling their children's lives.

And under the heading of being a good role model, parents should also take a look at their own schedule to see if they're overbooked. After all, 45 percent of stressed-out teens wish they could spend more time with their parents.

Adolescents' lack of time in high school and college is a consistently mentioned plague. For some, it stems from a desire to have a full résumé. Most midadolescents competing for spots in elite colleges and universities are well aware that the game is less about brainpower and more about tenacity and sheer determination.

Many become overstressed early in life. By the time many students reach the middle of their junior year of high school, they want (most of them say "need") more money, and almost always that means finding a job. Research has shown that getting even a part-time job adds exponentially to the level of stress and busyness in the life of a midadolescent.

As the American Psychological Association reports, students who work twenty or more hours a week during the school year are "more emotionally distressed, have poorer grades, are more likely to smoke cigarettes, and are more likely to become involved in other high-risk behaviors such as alcohol and drug use."

The Sources of Stress

Before determining the sources of stress, we need to define stress. Here's how David Elkind defined it: "Stress is any *unusual* demand

134

for adaptation that forces us to call on our energy reserves over and above that which we ordinarily expend and replenish in the course of a twenty-four-hour period."

In *The Hurried Child*, Elkind offers a stress test for children. A point system charts a child's stress level based on changes in his or her life. If a child's score in any given year is beyond 150 points, Elkind says he or she has a "better than average chance of showing some symptoms of stress. If your child's score was above 300, there is a strong likelihood he or she will experience a serious change in health and/or behavior."

Here are some of the stressors Elkind lists and their point values:

Parent dies	100
Parents divorce	73
Parents separate	65
Parent travels as part of job	63
Parent remarries	50
Parents reconcile	45
Mother goes to work	45
School difficulties	39
Threat of violence at school	31

These "stressors" are but a sampling of the kinds of things that induce stress and anxiety in the life of a child.

A popular assumption is that adolescents, being older and more streetwise than children, are less vulnerable to these and other stressors. But because of the added burdens of abandonment, social fragmentation, and being forced to live in layers, midadolescents are even more prone to stress, with fewer accumulated points needed to push them over the edge.

In my observation of midadolescent busyness, stress, and pressure, I noticed three areas of stress that took their toll on most students: the stress of success, home, and relationships. These pressure points, while perhaps not overwhelming for all students, seem to have a significant impact on the emotional equilibrium of most. Let's examine them in turn.

135

The Stress of Success

The pressure to succeed—whether in the classroom, on the athletic field, or in any other endeavor—is the source of much stress. The quest for success leads to an elusive but powerful sense that students are never quite good enough. When students do something well, they believe it's only a step toward adequate performance. But failure still stalks them at every turn.

I encountered few students who allowed themselves just to do their best in a given arena and then let the chips fall where they may. When someone did well on a test or had a great tennis match, the time for celebration was short-lived. The pressure to continue to reach loftier heights was the defining sentiment.

As one student remarked, acting as a spokesperson for several others in a small-group setting, "We feel an incredible pressure to succeed in every area, or it will all fall apart."

When I asked what specifically would fall apart, the group could not say, but they were convinced that the statement was nonetheless accurate. What they are striving for is not the thing itself but rather what they believe the accomplishment will bring with it. Performance, then, is not about the touchdown, the A, or a role in the school play. It is about how people will perceive them.

In other words, adolescents have learned that what matters is not who they are but what they do, or more pointedly, what they can point to and say, "Look at me! I am worthy of attention and affection." For most students, the accolades that seemed to really sink in went beyond a deed and focused on their intrinsic

Youth Culture Update

Growing Up Is Hard to Do

According to a recent *USA Today* study of girls and women between the ages of sixteen and twenty-five, more than half (54 percent) feel anxiety over the way they look, and 33 percent feel they look "hot" if they wear revealing clothing.

But these same women also want careers and families. In fact 76 percent want both. Nearly four in ten believe they're growing up too fast.

Our Overstressed Adolescents

Landon Lynch

When I encountered the section in *Hurt* on busyness and stress, I was forced to remove myself and evaluate the status of our Young Life students in this respect. A couple things stood out that demanded attention.

Primarily, I began to see the subtle resentment in the high schoolers I was around toward adults who, as the student in *Hurt* said, "just don't get it." Every adult seemed to these kids like just one more individual who was going to expect something from them that they would have to try to juggle by themselves.

I decided to approach some of these more removed and cynical students differently. After asking how they were and what they'd been up to (because it almost surely would be a long list), I simply said, "Whoa, people always talk about how you guys have it so easy and you don't!" The glazed look was gone from their eyes and for the first time these kids were engaged, not because someone took their load from them, but because someone acknowledged that they had a legitimate load.

Since then I have seen the same sort of statement transform the indifferent look of many disillusioned kids in my Club. Now there is not one Club Talk that I give in Young Life when I don't say in some way before concluding, "I get to spend a lot of time with you guys, and your lives aren't as simple as people like to think."

Landon Lynch works as Field Staff for Young Life in Aurora, Colorado, at Grandview High School. One of his driving passions is figuring out how to more clearly convey the gospel to this adolescent audience. He said *Hurt* was a great help in understanding his audience, his friends.

worth. And when they received praise of this nature, it seemed to diffuse some of the need to perform and the stress that came along with it.

Home Sweet Stress

Students' interactions with their parents can be a major source of stress. A fight with a mom, dad, or stepparent just as they are walking out the door can produce a brooding mood that lasts much of the day. They don't like to talk about it, but they are easily discouraged if there's an unresolved conflict at home.

Midadolescents desperately want what they know they cannot have. On one side, they want parents to be great, nonjudgmental friends who affirm everything they do and leave them alone. On the other, they want parents who care enough about them to be, well, parents.

Even midadolescent logic can, when summoned to do so, see that these two desires cannot coexist when it comes to parents. There is no way a parent can be caring and involved, both nurturing and drawing boundaries for the child, and at the same time be such a great pal and fan that the parent never interferes in the child's life. This paradox is nonetheless what a midadolescent believes is not only possible but also preferable. Perhaps this is the difference between what kids want/need/feel and what they know to be realistic?

The greatest rub occurs when parents invade the primary safe place of the midadolescent: the cluster. When parents invade this

Putting into Practice

Retreats That Really Retreat

Jeff Baxter

I sat with a group of high school students and adult leaders to discuss the future of our local church's student ministry. In the midst of the conversation, I asked the students what brought stress into their lives.

Their list was exhausting (and brought stress into my life). It went something like, "money, jobs, school, not sleeping, disappointing my parents, sports, acceptance, picking the right friends, staying friends, hurting God, trying to keep up with everything, what will happen after high school, using my time wisely, being bored, and myself."

I realized that day how times have changed and the level of stress has increased over the years for all adolescents. Their stress is very real and not any less real than adult tension. It is hard to slow an adolescent down long enough to have a meaningful conversation. Does it seem as though they are all ADD? They are too busy calling, texting, typing, studying, and running to stop and just rest.

As a result of this first meeting, we decided to take action against overhurried and overstressed adolescents. We asked ourselves questions like:

How can we help slow students down in our ministry environment?

How can we build slower and safer authentic community with our students?

How can we get more mature, Jesus-following adults around our students in more meaningful ways?

How do we teach students to slow down and inspire them to cope and take control of their own stress?

sacred place, kids panic. Therefore parents need to figure out when to exert influence over their child and when to back off. This is not easy for a parent or a child, and it can cause stress for both.

Relationship Stress

The most delicate and yet easily disguised source of stress for midadolescents is their desire to keep people happy. Midadolescents may not seem to care about how others react to them, but that is an act. Midadolescents care deeply about what others think of them.

Much of the time their self-focus and self-centeredness keep them from reading the cues available to them. They may wear

How do we make sure our local church does not contribute to the stress of our students?

Our leadership team took action by organizing a retreat. And to address stress, we focused on creating a Sabbath Retreat. We wanted to develop a space for students to actually slow down and learn about resting. Our ministry team just wanted to take the word *retreat* seriously.

The Sabbath Retreat was a lightly programmed weekend event at an off-site retreat center. We left on a Friday and returned Sunday. There were four big group sessions (Friday evening, Saturday morning, Saturday evening, and Sunday morning).

During these sessions, it was not about a speaker, dramas, entertainment, or a big band. The purpose was to equip and empower students in "sacred practices" like silence and solitude, which involved Scripture study and prayer. We leaned on authors Richard Foster, Dallas Willard, and other spiritual mentors for our material and taught on true Sabbath from Jesus's life, using the book of Hebrews and other Scriptures.

During the other large time blocks of the weekend (late nights and afternoons), we encouraged the students to take a nap, have healthy fun, get alone, talk if they liked, play a game, laugh, and enjoy life. We encouraged them to slow down, rest, and relax. Our team did not want to put all of our adult boundaries on the students with high-level entertaining and draining emotional programs. Actually, we wanted students to return home rested. It began as a once-a-year event but now is sometimes a biannual event.

So did the experiment work? Yes.

dismissal by an adult or a student they don't like as a badge of assertive honor, but inside, they know they're taking a risk and desperately want everyone to respect and affirm if not outright like them.

One day a student handed me a note after class that read: "The thing we worry about the most is not disappointing others."

The cynic in me recalled the student and the class, which was exceptionally rowdy and flippant. So I was tempted to dismiss the note as a sarcastic attempt to manipulate my research. Yet the next day I felt different about the intention of the note's author. It seemed to me that what I had read as callous indifference and even arrogant disregard was actually a test.

First, this experience fostered slowness and the kids loved it. Students do not always like to be entertained with bigger and better. Sometimes they just need to take a deep breath and live in the healthy habits God intended and Jesus modeled.

Second, this retreat built deep community with students and adults. There was time for longer and deeper conversations about the rhythms of an abundant life in Jesus. Without the rush of minute-by-minute retreat programming with students rushing off to the next activity, they could just sit next to a fireplace sipping hot cocoa with friends and adult leaders and let the conversation flow.

Third, we provided instant practice for silence and solitude through the teaching, resources, and time we provided the students. There was plenty of space for alone time with God and random small-group time.

For the last several years, the Sabbath Retreat has been a huge success for both high school and college students who are longing for space to slow down, rest, and hear the voice of God more clearly. I invite you to be countercultural in your student ministry and offer a slower, peace-filled, and restful retreat.

Jeff Baxter received his doctor of ministry degree from Fuller Theological Seminary and spends much of his time studying, writing, or investing in the next generation at Starbucks while sipping on a peppermint mocha. He has spent more than a decade in adolescent ministry, which includes speaking experience and extensive international ministry travel. His latest writing, with Youth Specialties and Zondervan, is *The Long Haul: Following Jesus into College and Beyond,* due to hit bookstores in February 2009. You can read his growth writings at www.sacredoutfitter.blogspot.com or contact him for speaking at www.ParenTeen.com. Jeff, his beautiful wife, Laurie, and adorable children, Lillian, Levi, and Lara, live in Indiana.

Stress Is a Universal Problem for Youth

Jeffrey Spainhour

Having worked with middle and high school students on both coasts, I see some differences—country versus punk music, for example. I have also observed many similarities, an obvious one being high stress levels. Not only do I consistently see stress in youth, the stress they feel comes from many directions.

Crying, vigorous pacing, running their hands through their hair like they want to pull it out, even the "grrr" that comes from deep within are but a few expressions I have experienced from this overstressed youth culture. We may see this so much that it actually seems normal. Is it? Is this the life Jesus intended?

After a few days in Kenya, a young man was excited that we were finally starting the building project that was planned, but his anxiety grew as he learned there was a cultural difference in the understanding of time. I explained that he was not really there to build the building.

"What?" he asked with confusion and anger. "Then why did I raise all this money and fly halfway around the world?"

I explained that he was there to build relationships, not a physical structure. Our culture has become so oriented on producing something that can be seen and measured, we have lost sight of important things we may not be able to see.

Over and over, I see confused priorities. We feel success only when we are rewarded with what we can experience in a concrete way (or show to others for

Did I really care about what they thought or, more important, about them? Was I interested in each one as a unique and valuable person or was I one more adult who was willing to use and exploit them for my career?

When I recognized what was at the core of their response to me, I saw twenty-eight fragile midadolescents who wanted to know that they mattered to me. This was a class that was really tough, so the tone was the class's tone toward me and each other, causing me to be cynical. I was the teacher, and they were jerks. Then this kid handed me a sincere-sounding note, that at first I dismissed because of his particular behavior in that class. The more I thought about it, however, the more I realized that even in the midst of chaos and disrespect, the kids were craving my interest and even affection. What a gift that note was!

affirmation). This mind-set enforces the teaching of our culture's definition of what success and importance look like and locks us into looking for the next thing we can build or do to be valued or to simply show the number of things on our schedule that mark our busyness, thus pointing to the conclusion that we must be valued and important.

Not only are youth (and their parents) always on the go, but also all too often the church adds to this cycle. I met with a group of middle school parents and asked how many of them were at the church more then three times a week. Most hands went up. In providing ample opportunities for our youth and parents to be involved, are we adding to their busyness? How can we encourage times of Sabbath?

When I have asked young people, "What does it mean to follow Christ?" consistently they answer, "Read the Bible, pray, be nice, go to church and youth group." Very few answers reflect an understanding that grace from God is just that, from God, not earned by what we do.

Our culture's influence on our understanding of God is producing a works-based understanding of grace. This way of thinking adds to the stress of today's youth, putting God out of reach and causing them to feel inadequate. Constantly moving from one thing to another impedes the formation of deeper relationships, resulting in many of today's teens feeling lonely and insecure.

Today's parents and youth are growing up in a time when there are many opportunities and a philosophy of, if you can do it, then "just do it." Youth leaders, parents,

Delayed Development

As I watched their frazzled busyness, their burden of multiple layers of expectations, their overlapping and competing commitment to activities, and their desire to access and utilize the latest technologies, I could not help but feel that midadolescents have been backed into a difficult corner.

On the one hand, a major aspect of their developmental responsibility is to learn how to cope with stress and manage their emotions. On the other hand, adults have continued to pile on them increased burdens and complex demands. What occurs when these two competing forces clash? Midadolescents feel the need to flee from both the pressures and their responsibility to cope. This

and students have told me for years they are tired and too busy, and if they feel they are not busy and "productive," they feel guilty.

We need to continue to hold in front of youth and their parents the truth that we need to be quiet. God teaches this often in his Word. Scriptural truths need to be reopened. We need to remember Psalm 46:10: "Be still, and know that I am God"; and Psalm 23, which shows our Lord making us lie down in green pastures and leading us beside still waters to restore our soul.

Numbers 20:1–13 shows God's people making an unprecedented journey and having life-or-death stress, wondering how they would get food and water. During this time, Moses and Aaron went away from the large crowd to be still and pray.

When the Israelites reached the Red Sea while running from the Egyptians, God told them, "You need only to be still" (Exod. 14:14)

Jesus, after he fed the five thousand, sent the crowd away (Matt. 14:13–23). He knew it was important for him to have a quiet time in solitude.

God still speaks in a still quiet voice. Do we have time to hear him? Are we available to God? We need to live out and teach the necessity of being still.

Jeffrey Spainhour has been working with youth since 1992. He received his master of divinity degree from Fuller Theological Seminary and is Associate Pastor at Triangle Presbyterian Church in Durham, North Carolina. Jeff is the cofounder and cochairman of Staff of Hope, a community development ministry focused on the people of Kenya and Tanzania, www.staffofhope.org.

becomes one more factor—sometimes the deciding factor—in the creation and sustenance of the world beneath.

Mary Pipher wrote about this problem in her bestselling book *Reviving Ophelia*, arguing that adolescent girls (and I would certainly add boys) "need good habits for coping with stress." She went on to explain that adults must teach and train the young how to handle the stress of everyday life.

Perhaps there is some truth in the concept that development ultimately comes down to the individual journey of an adolescent, but the search for a satisfying and unique identity that includes the abilities to cope with and manage stress and emotions also has a great deal to do with one's environment.

As Patricia Hersch wrote in her book *A Tribe Apart: A Journey into the Heart of American Adolescents*:

What kids need from adults is not just rides, pizza, chaperones, and discipline. They need the telling of stories, the close, ongoing contact, so that they can learn to be accepted. If nobody is there to talk to, it is difficult to get the lessons of your own life so that you are adequately prepared to do the next thing. Without a link across generations, kids will only hear from their peers. . . . In national surveys and focus groups, America's youth have given voice to serious longing. They want more regular contact with adults who care about and respect them.

Midadolescence is a period when even those youth who believe in themselves have difficulty with the multiple layers of expectation placed on them. Today's strongest midadolescents face challenges

Our Adolescents Are Watching Us

Dudley Chancey

For years social scientists have warned us about bad stress or "pileup." Normal stress is not bad, but when we become overstressed, as Clark points out in this chapter, we are in danger of breaking.

Did you find yourself adding up the points in your life or your child's life based on Elkind's list of stressors? The research that Clark shares about stress in adolescents' lives sounds very familiar. The three areas of stress that Clark mentions (success, home, and relationships) take their toll on many students trying to navigate the journey of adolescence.

Our busy culture in the United States is demanding. One has to run to keep up. Clark mentions that we adults have backed today's adolescents into a corner with increased burdens and complex demands. To be honest, parents are caught up in the same economic culture and society and they too are constantly running to stay ahead. Adults fail many times to be the examples that adolescents need.

Clark closes the chapter pointing out that many of today's adolescents are hiding behind the mask of busyness. Perhaps this is all a mad cycle. A student is lonely because his or her parents are caught up in the cycle of producing to get more, so they aren't around to teach their children even the basic life skills. The students do what their greatest role models (parents) do. They get busy. They get meaningless jobs. They join clubs. They play every sport. They play every instrument. They skate. They paint. They draw. They write. They hurt. Most parents applaud this "work." Clark points out that if they work and/or play hard enough, the hurt will be numbed or go away. But they must

that their parents (and even their older brothers and sisters) did not. Those who possess the strongest self-efficacy beliefs, and therefore have a greater ability to handle whatever the environment throws at them, still face periods of struggle, insecurity, and stress.

The Mask of Busyness

Just below the surface, today's midadolescents feel a sense of loneliness and isolation that betrays the confidence with which they present themselves, even to one another.

The busyness they embrace keeps them from having to reflect on their dreams, their relationships, and their lives. The resul-

move quickly or they will be found out. They hear, "Knock it out of the park, Son," and "You go, Girl!" when they are listening—straining—to hear, "You matter to me."

As mentors, teachers, ministers, and parents, we can address this reality with the adolescents in our sphere of influence. Perhaps the first thing we need to address is our calendars and schedules. Getting rid of some of the busyness that causes much of the overstress in our lives is a must. This will allow more time to deal with true success, the home front, and all other relationships. We know from research that adolescents get overstressed with girlfriend/boyfriend relationships, arguments with parents, trouble with siblings, trouble with classmates, arguments between parents—especially over financial matters.

Another way parents can convey to their adolescents that they are a valued part of the family is to help them identify with the family heritage. The more we know about where we come from (our family of origin), the more confident we are. I use the following on parent/teen retreats and in my college classes. I ask participants/students to complete a genogram. This assignment demands that they sit with their family and gather information about their family's history and how they have dealt with relationships. They trace relationship patterns in birth and marriage and they trace their faith heritage. It is amazing to me how many parents have never told their children their faith journey. Once again, researchers tell us that the more an adolescent knows about his or her family and its history, the better potential they have to deal successfully with overstress that comes from the home front.

We as mentors, teachers, parents, and youth workers can help adolescents by equipping them with coping skills, communication skills (talking and listening), and problem-solving skills. We must have unconditional love and well-defined limits to go

tant stress serves only to compound the desperation they feel that somehow, in some way, they might be able to work hard enough or play hard enough to free themselves from the burden of loneliness and fear.

Certainly, they are tired, and many are angry. Both of these feelings, however, are symptoms of a deeper threat to their well-being and ultimately to their ability to progress through midadolescence. At their core, they long for the safety and freedom of childhood and have no clear vision of what adulthood will be like. As a result of the abandonment they have faced throughout their lives, most midadolescents carry inside them a powerful defense mechanism that keeps them running as fast and as hard as they can. They

along with these skills, and we adults must model these skills in our own lives as well. Our adolescents are watching us and doing what we do—good or bad.

Finally, those of us who work with adolescents know that if we equip parents to do their jobs better, everyone wins. One can Google "teen stress" and get hundreds of articles and suggestions on how to deal with this issue, including the following. We should teach parents how to:

- encourage their teen to talk about what he or she is going through and be willing to listen
- offer reassurance, encouragement, and support
- continue to provide structure, stability, and predictability
- encourage their teen to participate in activities normally enjoyed
- model effective stress management and coping skills
- build a relationship so their teen feels comfortable coming to them when he or she needs help

Other useful hints from the medical world include the following: Help your teen to exercise and eat a proper diet; avoid caffeine, alcohol, illegal drugs, and tobacco; relax; be assertive in expressing how he or she feels; be positive; learn to accept something less than perfection; and maintain a network of positive friendships.

Dudley Chancey teaches youth ministry and family studies at Oklahoma Christian University in Edmond, Oklahoma. Besides being at Oklahoma Christian University part of the year, he spends his time in Honduras (www.silvermm.org) and planning youth conferences (www.winterfest.org) and youth ministry conferences (www.ncym.org).

know no other way to cope with life. The quicker they move, the less vulnerable they are to ridicule, critique, or even examination. Midadolescents know they must put on a mask of confidence, even arrogance, or they will be chewed up by those who would find them out.

The adults who love and care for them should not be fooled. Yes, they are busy. Yes, they are stressed. But in the midst of their blur, they want someone—you or me—to take a break from our adult form of busyness long enough to show them through our words and actions the one thing they want to hear from us: "You matter to me."

10

in search of ethics and morality

In 2007 Junior Achievement released its fifth annual Teen Ethics survey, which was filled with interesting and, for many, disheartening results. While 71 percent of teens polled felt they were ready and able to make ethical decisions once they hit the workforce, nearly four in ten—38 percent—also felt that lying, cheating, and even committing acts of violence were sometimes necessary to succeed.

"The high percentages of teenagers who freely admit that unethical behavior can be justified is alarming," said David Miller, executive director of the Yale Center for Faith and Culture and a professor of business ethics. "It suggests an attitude of ethical relativism and rationalization of whatever actions serve one's immediate needs and purposes."

But while Miller and other experts may be alarmed, what I saw during my time with teens is how *un-alarming* unethical behavior has become in their world. In fact it is mundane. It is the new norm.

The New Norm

Contemporary midadolescents pass much of their thought processes through the filter of self-interest and self-protection. They see themselves as having been abandoned and left on their own to navigate the complexities of life. Living like this has had an impact on how they view right and wrong.

As we have seen, today's teens are cursed by a profound sense that the adults in their lives have abandoned them. As a result, they are focused on living life in ways that promote their safety and security. Often this means they pursue the pleasures of the moment without the ethical concerns of some adults, but that's not because they believe ethics are irrelevant. Rather, they are preoccupied with immediate pleasures because they want to create for themselves a world that makes life easier, safer, and more satisfying.

Does that mean they have become lawless and have discarded any commitment to ethical rules and standards? Not at all. Today's adolescents believe ethics are still important. They realize that no society can possibly survive without an ethical framework that helps its members define and order life's choices.

The ethical systems of teens are a revised version of the predominant ethics of the larger culture. For example, even though many teens are concerned about lying, stealing, and cheating, these are not the focus of their ethical systems. Instead, teens place a premium on *loyalty* (which is primarily defined as loyalty to friends and cluster, but occasionally also involving loyalty to one teacher over another, their school, or their community). They also value staying within the preordained *boundaries* of social life (such as where to sit, whom to date, what activities to participate in).

These and other simple, straightforward, and easily negotiated ethical parameters of adolescent life make up the ethical scaffolding of midadolescence today. As a result, more traditional (or adult) standards covering lying or stealing have only a secondary relevance for midadolescents. It is not that they reject some of these traditional ethical categories. It's just that these issues assume less significance when placed in competition with the standards that adolescents have come to regard as more urgent or more important.

Or as one expert put it: "They [adolescents] have been hardened by today's realities. They have seen an acceptance of disposing of ethics and morals if it serves a need. They see it is OK to do what you want to do as long as you meet your personal requirements."

Cheat Sheets

Several polls suggest that youth today are more willing to cheat than their parents were, and they're less likely to think there's much wrong with it. And, with a rash of cheating scandals rocking various schools across the country, it looks like all those polls may be on to something.

Last month, several students at Chapel Hill (North Carolina) High School were caught cheating in various ways. One used a master key to break into a teacher's office and swipe an AP history test. Another took a picture of an upcoming test with his cell phone. At a New Hampshire high school, students broke into a file cabinet to snag an AP math test. And at an elite school in Los Angeles, several students were suspended for distracting teachers in order to steal Spanish and history tests.

"Academic misconduct is small potatoes in the moral domain, compared to murder, rape and drug abuse," said Jason Stephens, an assistant professor of educational psychology at the University of Connecticut. "But the cheating epidemic is kind of death by a thousand cuts. Ultimately, it undermines the self when the moral self should be growing."

Adult Hypocrisy

A contributing reason for all ethical uncertainty is that kids are growing up in a world where adults rarely live up to their own ethical rhetoric. Adolescents have grown up in a world in which adults say one thing and do another. We even have a saying for this: "Do as I say, not as I do!" The young, therefore, have learned from the example of adults how little selfless ethical standards mean.

Examples of adults' unethical behavior can be seen on a daily basis in the worlds of government, business, entertainment, and sports—where a foul is not a foul until it is called (or the player is "caught"). Kids have grown up in a culture that, on the one hand, values "playing by the rules" while also praising those people who can skirt the rules to their benefit.

At times it seems as though teens behave with a combination of inconsistency and defensive relativism. Erin Curry, a researcher who tried to interpret the seemingly conflicting data about teen ethics, put it this way: "On some political issues involving religion, America's youth seem to be more conservative than their elders, but cheating, stealing and lying by high school students have increased with alarming vigor."

Adults who want to understand the world of midadolescents must learn where the ethical lines are drawn and what adolescents consider ethical or moral issues.

This chapter examines two areas in which adolescents view ethics much differently than adults do (or at least differently than adults *say* they do). Specifically we will look at lying and cheating. These are not the only ethical issues in which adolescents function differently than adults, but they do illustrate teens' sustained, regular, and even daily rejection of the ethical priorities of the adults who raised and trained them.

When it comes to adolescent ethics, issues such as sexuality, alcohol, drugs, justice, racism, and a myriad of other topics are viewed through a similar pragmatic, self-protective lens.

Lies: From White to Bald-Faced

There are all kinds of approaches to lying among today's teens, as I quickly found out when I sat down and talked to them.

"Everybody lies, and everybody knows that everybody lies," said a junior girl from rural North Carolina.

"Is it wrong to lie?" I asked.

"It depends," she went on. "If it doesn't really hurt anybody, and it is necessary for any reason, a 'white lie' is not really a lie, and then it's not wrong."

Some people call this relativism. Others call it pragmatism. I suppose the precise classification depends on the motives of the one doing the lying and the social context.

"So, does everybody really lie?" I asked, "even to their parents or ministers?"

"Especially to our parents and pastors!" she told me. "They can't be trusted with anything!"

I heard variations on this theme throughout my study. Or as the girl I talked to put it: "Everybody lies, and everybody knows that everybody lies."

When I told the students involved with my study that part of my research would focus on adolescent lying behaviors, they looked at me as if I had said that I'd be studying whether adolescents breathe. Lying, especially as defined by adults, has become one more natural reflex of daily living.

And besides, they'd say, it's not even really lying! All students, when they find themselves in a position in which a lie would be the easiest route to self-protection, will lie just as easily as the next kid. Pervasive and unchecked lying has become a central reality to almost every midadolescent in our culture.

Self-Protection

Studies on adolescents and truth telling have found that as few as 5 percent of adolescents say they never lied to parents about where they were. These studies also revealed that girls lie more

Youth Culture Update

On My Honor

Responding to their peers' growing willingness to cheat and plagiarize, some students at the University of Texas at San Antonio proposed a new honor code for the school. Only one problem: a good chunk of the code's wording seems to match that of Brigham Young University's honor code—and never gives the Utah school proper attribution.

San Antonio students say it was an honest mistake, but experts believe it's a sign of the times.

"That's the consequence of the Internet and the availability of things," said Daniel Wueste, director of the Rutland Institute for Ethics at Clemson University in South Carolina. "It doesn't feel like what would be in a book. You Google it and here it comes."

to parents about sex, and more often to their dads, than do boys. Boys lie more often than girls to their moms. But both genders are pretty good at it. Only 5 percent said they were often caught in their dishonesty.

I observed that the most regular defense offered for lying to authority figures, like parents, teachers, and coaches, was explained in terms of a perceived need to protect oneself or one's friends. In incident after incident, most teens said they lied to avoid being punished for something that, in general, they didn't believe was wrong. One student put it this way: "Most things are kept from my parents because of the repercussions."

Rarely did I encounter a midadolescent who believed that lying was inherently unethical. Midadolescents reshape the idea of lying to the point where a justified deception, including an outright, bald-faced lie, is not actually lying. Nearly every student admitted to lying regularly, without remorse. Yet many of these same students believe that they are highly moral, ethical, and honest people! According to one study, when teens were asked whether each was "basically an honest person," 85 percent of teens surveyed said yes. It's a typical string of logic that I heard again and again: "I lie, sure. So does everybody else. But I'm an honest person, though, and that's what really counts."

The Anatomy of an Excuse

One day an athlete explained to me that when a coach asked why he was late for practice, he made up a semiplausible but fabricated story. As he told me what he had done, he made no attempt to conceal or even justify it to me. In fact he shared it with me as if it were the most natural and normal thing in the world.

When I pressed him, asking him how he could defend his deception, he looked at me with near amazement.

"Coach would have made a big deal out of it, and it wasn't a big deal," he told me. "He didn't deserve to know the truth."

"But you lied to him," I said. "Isn't that wrong?"

"I didn't lie, exactly. I just didn't think it was his business to know my business."

"What happens," I went on, "if that same coach told you that you were going to start next week, and then he turned around and

154

had someone else start in your place? Let's say he was trying to motivate you, and it worked, and you figured out later that he never really intended to have you start. Is that wrong? Is that a lie?"

"Obviously," he told me. "No coach can lie like that, especially to a kid. That's wrong!"

The more I tried to tie these two events together, the less this young man was either interested or able to connect the dots. To him, a lie was not wrong unless it was done to him. When I shared this story with adolescents around the country, it was clear that to some his statement reflected an ethical infraction, but to many others it did not. And even those who saw the inconsistency still believed the guy was right.

After speaking at one conference, where I talked about teen perceptions of lying, one adolescent wrote to me on the subject. "I lie because I have never truly found a person to be honest with," he said. "Mostly I lie because I find it likely that any feelings I may convey to that person would eventually come back to haunt me, whether my parents, or even my friends, school, or church. I just can't trust anybody, so I need to protect myself. If I have to lie now and then to do that, so be it."

Despite the behavior, flippancy, and defensive rationalizing of midadolescents, lying does represent an important ethical issue for them, and when pressed, most of them do "get" the difficulty of their position. The issue for them is that the morality regarding truth telling is a second-tier ethic, meaning that while it is an important and necessary ethic on which any society is built, such overarching realities may be placed on "developmental hold" when the more immediate need to protect oneself (or one's friends) is encountered.

Making (or Faking) the Grade

If lying is dishonesty, cheating is dishonesty in an academic setting. And according to Michael Josephson of the Josephson Institute of Ethics, it's an activity that is sweeping across teen culture:

> The evidence is that a willingness to cheat has become the norm and that parents, teachers, coaches and even religious educators

155

have not been able to stem the tide. The scary thing is that so many kids are entering the workforce to become corporate executives, politicians, airplane mechanics and nuclear inspectors with the dispositions and skills of cheaters and thieves.

Research shows that cheating increases during middle and late adolescence, and that students blame their cheating on others, including teachers, parents, the school, or even society at large. In one study, researchers found that high school students were far more carefree and casual about cheating than were college students. This supports the notion that midadolescents, by developmental definition, do not seem to give much energy to ethical issues that don't provide immediate self-promotion or protection.

Putting into Practice

Establishing Ethical Role Models

Mindy Coates Smith

Recently one of the most prominent (and expensive!) private high schools in Los Angeles expelled six tenth-grade students responsible for an elaborate cheating scandal that involved stealing midterm exams and distributing them to classmates.

The school is nationally known for its reputation of stellar academics, and many adults in the community were shocked by the students' apparent lack of integrity. This story perked my interest particularly, as a handful of students who attend this school also attend the youth programs at my church. As youth leaders, how do we address this ethical imbalance with students and families? Over the last few years, our ministry has wrestled with many of these ethical conundrums and has developed a couple of helpful responses.

From Bill Clinton to Enron to Young Hollywood, our students have not had the best role models from which to glean a moral compass. Even some of the adults they are close to in their own lives promote questionable ethical decisions, such as the coach who bends the rules to win or the teacher who turns a blind eye to continuous cheating. In response, our ministry has felt the need to provide students with a rich group of helpful examples.

We have developed a team of responsible, loving adult volunteer leaders to serve as another voice in students' lives. Each leader is encouraged to be directly active in the lives of four to six students and families, emailing, calling, attending games, and

And as I found in my talks with young people, the very definition of cheating varied from person to person, situation to situation. For instance, if a teacher was well liked and was seen as honest, respectful, and fair, then most students would self-police themselves, decreasing the amount of cheating in that class. But if another teacher "unfairly" gave a pop quiz, then whoever felt the need to cheat was only giving that teacher what he or she deserved.

In another situation, when a student who was relatively respected felt that he or she had the right to cheat for one reason or another, it was up to the class to protect and defend that student's choice. But if another student who, for whatever reason, was not seen as a peer ally and chose to cheat, that student would be turned in (this was actually quite rare, but it happened now and then).

so on, so as to increase their ability to be an example in the students' lives (not a small request, especially for a commuter environment like Los Angeles!). We spend extensive amounts of time training and meeting with leaders through monthly staff meetings, one-on-ones, training weekends, and leader mission trips.

It's not an easy task to recruit these leaders (as anyone in middle school ministry knows, it's hard enough to get someone to lead a seventh grade guys small group for a week, much less a year!). And training and nurturing these leaders continuously can feel like an enormous strain of time and resources for the paid staff, but we recognize that this is a vitally important part of our ministry. Empowering the volunteers means giving up control of my own desired ministry outcomes in favor of a more organic system in which we all share a part of the process.

Besides role models, we have seen that another major factor in the apparent breakdown of teenage ethics is the current hurriedness of fragmented families. Busy adults are parenting busy kids whose lives are strewn throughout classrooms, athletic facilities, vehicles, and sometimes more than one household. Given these factors and the enormous outside pressure to "succeed," can we really be surprised that cheating, lying, and stealing have become a way of life for most students? Potentially the usual adult reaction of harsh discipline and shame furthers the systemic abandonment that is a large part of the problem in the first place.

In response, our church has formed a fellowship group for parents of teenagers. We noticed a lot of support for parents of toddlers and preschoolers, but nothing for parents with older kids. We now have a group that meets once a month in which a

My own research confirmed the findings of Donald McCabe, a professor of management at Rutgers University and founder of the Center for Academic Integrity at Duke University, who has written about academic dishonesty. These are some of the comments of midadolescents he recorded:

> I think times have changed. Cheating is kind of considered, I don't know, just a kind of daily thing that's out there, almost kind of acceptable. Teachers know it and students know it. . . . It's almost a big deal if you don't cheat. . . . There are times when you just are in need of a little help. . . . You can't change that; you can't change people wanting to get the A or whatever. . . . If cheating is going to get you the grade, then that's the way to do it.

speaker will present a topic relevant to parents (such as teenage ethics) and then break into discussion groups so that parents can learn from each other and build relationships at the same time. Many parents are unaware of the cultural landscape their adolescents operate in, and therefore this open dialogue helps them focus their attention, and may create the impetus for the all-important discussion at home. We have found this to be a very effective way to not only communicate vital information, but also to support and love parents through this tricky time of parenting.

The world students live in is almost too complicated and messy for across-the-board rules. The situations and scenarios they encounter each day require a sophisticated set of reasoning and valuing capabilities, tools they are just beginning to develop. I think one of the greatest things we can do as a community of adults is to teach students discernment within wider set boundaries. We need to help them make decisions using a biblically based set of values (that we discuss often in our relationships with students). Ultimately this discernment comes from a continued, deeper understanding of God. Therefore part of our role is to create opportunities for students to experience God so that their decisions can be made from a place of relationship instead of rule.

May we have the courage to make good decisions in our own lives and have the endurance to walk alongside these students to steer them toward discerning, God-honoring choices.

Currently Mindy Coates Smith serves as Codirector of Middle School Discipleship at Bel Air Presbyterian Church in Los Angeles, where she works alongside her husband, RO. Together they contribute to a youth ministry blog: www.collectionofcrumbs.wordpress.com

In a nationally publicized study conducted by the Josephson Institute of Ethics in the fall of 2002, researchers found that

> stealing and lying by high school students have continued their alarming, decade-long upward spiral. A survey of 12,000 high school students showed that students admitting they cheated on an exam at least once in the past year jumped from 61 percent in 1992 to 74 percent in 2002. . . . The percentage who say they lied to their teachers and parents also increased substantially.

Traditionally cheating has been defined as allowing someone to look at and copy your work without stopping them as well as not reporting it. If we applied a broad definition that included these approaches to cheating, I believe the number of cheaters would probably be above 90 percent today.

An example of adolescents' inconsistent understanding of the ethics related to cheating is found in one student's letter to the editor of the *Los Angeles Times*, which had published an article about the Josephson Institute report:

> I am an A student. I budget my time, even though I have basketball practice and don't arrive home from my bus ride until 6 p.m. But I have had friends tell me that they didn't study or they didn't know how to do the work or didn't try. They anticipate that the kid next to them studied, and they look at that student's paper. I have on occasion knowingly let someone copy from my paper. It was a smart kid who went blank on a question. I know he studied, so I put my paper to the edge so that he could get a look.
>
> Some say that it is not cheating if you don't get caught. But to me, cheating is cheating, for you are cheating yourself of an opportunity to learn.

Plagiarism, another form of cheating, is not even seen by most kids as cheating. Technology is a major factor in teens' widespread lack of concern about plagiarism. Donald McCabe notes that the Internet has provided an unprecedented opportunity for plagiarism: "Copying a few lines from an obscure website into one's own term paper is not defined by many students as plagiarism," and more than 70 percent of college students do not consider such an act "serious cheating."

I believe an almost perfect storm of unethical scholastic behavior can occur when three factors converge:

- The world is one in which adults and even the media portray relativism as the ethic of the day.
- Ethics are related to self-interest, self-protection, and relational loyalty instead of to rhetorically affirmed moral standards.
- The Internet offers a seriously tempting option for getting information for less work.

Does the Punishment Fit the Crime?

Like lying, cheating is clearly widespread and there are no signs of it abating. Many say that we, as a culture, have reached a point at which cheating is an offense only when one gets caught. Students in my study admitted as much. If someone gets hurt or if someone gets caught cheating, then that person is wrong. In the interim, however, the chorus keeps singing, "What is the big deal? So I cheat, so what?"

The adolescent world is filled with its own deceptive and unethical practices, but in my conversations with students, they were reluctant to talk about how such breaches of trust are dealt with in the midadolescent community. As I unintentionally bumped into scenarios, I was allowed a glimpse of how this behavior is handled.

In general, when there is a violation of trust within a cluster or between friends, a flurry of accusation and counteraccusation takes place, followed by intense neutral party negotiations intended to heal the rift as quickly and as painlessly as possible. In the cases I observed, the conflict subsided as quickly as it erupted, with as little public fanfare as possible. A close group of friends is so committed to maintaining the status quo of stable, familylike relationships that the system will not allow an ethical conflict to fester.

I did witness an exception to this when a guy felt he was being pulled to choose between his girlfriend and his cluster. The crowning blow occurred when the cluster perceived that he had lied to them to spend time with his girlfriend. This incident was quickly handled and seemed to blow over, but the sin was not wholly forgiven. Some of the guys in his cluster felt he had violated a sacred ethic—the sanctity of the cluster. Responses ranged from cold shoulders to outright ostracism. In this particular case, the cluster ultimately found a way for him to have a girlfriend and to stay friends.

Lessons in Fudging

In the film *The Emperor's Club*, actor Kevin Kline plays William Hundert, a private school teacher who fudges the grade of a student to do the boy a favor. Although Hundert was attempting to motivate this wayward student, the boy later cheats during a public competitive exam. Later the boy grows into a man who functions as a world-class cheater and views the world as a place in which it is perfectly acceptable to take any shortcut to get by.

When Hundert realizes that his own cheating had hurt another student by denying that student's right to participate in the finals of the competition, he apologizes to the spurned student. The irony of the film is that the cheating of the adult teacher empowered the cheating of the first student—an issue that was never resolved.

The Emperor's Club is a poignant reminder of how our society has arrived at its current ethical morass. To point fingers at the young for their relativism and deception is to display a naïveté of the worst kind.

Our efforts at stopping the ethical slide of the young have not worked. We may try slogans to reinforce ethical values, such as the "ref in your head" advertising campaign designed to discourage academic cheating, but until we are willing to match our own societal ethics, values, and moral choices with those to which we tell our youth to aspire, we will not be able to affect their ethical processes.

A system of ethics is operating in the world of midadolescents. Unfortunately, it is filled with inconsistency, self-centered justice, and relativistic ethical opportunism. If adults commit to train the young to care for others instead of just themselves and reinforce this view with commitment to integrity and honesty, then we have the best chance of influencing their moral development in a positive way.

11

I party, therefore I am

Way back in 1980 (which is an eternity ago in pop culture terms), the Police released an album featuring a song that pretty well summarizes many of the attitudes of today's teens toward partying. The song was entitled "When the World Is Winding Down, You Make the Best of What's Still Around."

One result of the feelings of abandonment that many teens experience is that they party recklessly in an effort to fill or medicate the hunger in their soul. Or as one girl told me: "Everybody I know drinks and drinks a lot."

When I first heard this statement, I was not surprised. After all, I was aware that my source was a well-known partyer. But when I heard it from three other kids (a sophomore girl who described herself as "religious," a freshman girl in the school chorale, and a quiet junior boy who seemed to be limited in his ability to cross social boundaries), I began to wonder if this was a more widespread trend than I had assumed.

In our society, alcohol consumption and the recreational use of marijuana have always been viewed as dangerous and destructive behaviors for adolescents. Adults have attempted to educate, inform, and threaten adolescents to keep them from drinking and smoking marijuana. But things are complicated by a double standard: adults consume a great deal of alcohol, and as popular TV shows, like *Weeds,* reveal, many also smoke marijuana.

It was with these thoughts in mind that I sought to gain a first-hand understanding of how midadolescents use or abuse alcohol and recreational drugs (primarily tobacco and marijuana). Here's what I found.

Everybody Does It—or Do They?

I wanted to test the claim of the girl who told me: "Everybody I know drinks and drinks a lot." Depending on the cluster being discussed, this may be an overstatement, but not by as much as most adults believe. When it comes to substance use and abuse, midadolescents fall into one of two categories:

- The first is comprised of the vast majority of students who drink and smoke almost exclusively at social events—either among small groups of friends or at a party.

Youth Culture Update

Rural Teens
More Likely to Drink

Think farm towns are wholesome and big cities pits of temptation? When it comes to alcohol, think again. A study done by the federal Substance Abuse and Mental Health Services Administration indicates that seven of the top ten areas for underage binge drinking (five or more drinks at a time) are in Wyoming, Montana, and the Dakotas. The worst region of all is south-central Wyoming, where the population density is a meager five people for every square mile. In fact 30 percent of youth in that region binge drink—more than twice the national average.

On average, rural youth are twice as likely to binge drink as youth from urban areas.

- The second is made up of adolescents who use alcohol and/ or drugs while alone or perhaps with one other person. This group is smaller, and those who fall into this category are often outcasts.

When it comes to the social partyer, it became clear to me that if one member of a cluster drinks, we can assume one of the following:

1. All the members drink.
2. The drinker is aberrant, and the rest of the cluster refrains from alcohol use.
3. Most members of the cluster drink, but one or even a few do not.

Here's what each of these three scenarios looks like.

Everybody In!

This is the most common situation. When one member of a cluster drinks (or smokes tobacco and/or marijuana), the rest also tend to drink at roughly the same rate. This is true even if one or more members of the cluster did not drink when the cluster was being formed. The cluster made the decision, however (probably without much or any discussion), and those in the cluster make a real commitment to the cluster's consensus.

The philosophy for these party animals was summarized on the high school chat room www.futazi.com: "No matter how many stupid things you do while drinking (except driving, etc.), it's all worthwhile. Knockin' back beers with your best buds is the way to go."

Some Do, Some Don't

A cluster may be basically committed to refraining from alcohol, but it may lower that commitment to include someone who drinks. It appears that most of the time this deviation was present when the cluster was formed, and therefore, members implicitly acknowledged that this behavior would not be seen as deviant. In this case, the cluster may seem to be committed to a corporate ethic that excludes drinking, but in reality, the decision whether to drink is left up to each member.

165

Youth Using Cold Meds to Get High

The U.S. government says that more than three million youth between ages twelve and twenty-five have used cold and cough medicine to get high—about the same amount as have used LSD and far more than have used methamphetamines.

That equates to more than 5 percent of United States youth, according to the federal Substance Abuse and Mental Health Services Administration 2006 survey. The survey also revealed that 82 percent of these meds-abusing teens also used marijuana.

Most Do, Others Don't

When members of a cluster are actively involved in alcohol consumption, it is understandable to assume that the cluster has an ethic that supports it. Anyone who chooses to deviate from this expectation, as the logic goes, would suffer from peer pressure to conform. But this is not necessarily the case. Things get tricky when a member, for whatever reason, decides to break from the established norms of the cluster. At such times, the cluster and the member have to make a decision. Do we allow the person to discard a previously agreed-on value and find a way to accommodate this change or do we go through the pain and struggle of banishing the offender from the cluster?

The cluster is the safest possible community in the life of a midadolescent. This implies that, at least on the surface, the cluster is expected to flex with the changes of individual members. Cluster groups hold cohesion and unity as higher values—especially during the first year or two of forming—than the specific behavior of individual members. Exceptions to this would be those behaviors that are destructive to the cluster itself (such as a new relationship that violates many of the cluster values) or are a vast departure from the norms of the cluster (such as moving from drinking to hard drug use). It is rare, however, for a cluster to choose dismissal when confronted with a relatively minor shift.

My overall impression is that the rules concerning substance use (other than hard drugs) rarely jeopardize the integrity of the group. Almost across the board, clusters typically fall into an "It's okay if you use alcohol or marijuana and okay if you don't" arrangement. Accommodation is a small price to pay in comparison to throwing up for grabs the negotiated rules, ethics, and norms of a cluster.

Inside Today's "Animal House"

When the United States Library of Congress chose films it deemed "culturally significant" for preservation in the National Film Registry, one of the movies that made the list was 1978's *Animal House*, which is also one of the most profitable movies of all time (in part because it was made on a tiny budget of 2.7 million dollars). The film shows that college parties have been the stuff of legends for decades. High school parties have also become notorious, as we saw in 1983's *Risky Business* with Tom Cruise.

High school parties have been depicted in film, on television, in advertisements, and through music ever since an adolescent subculture became a part of the social landscape. Nearly all mid-adolescents want to party and they are going to party regardless of what parents say. It has been ingrained in the narrative of the population and therefore it goes with the territory of being a mid-adolescent in this culture.

Unfortunately, the party scene is not really about parties at all. It is about drinking and, to a certain degree, drug use, sexual play, and other risky behaviors. Far too many students believe that it's simply impossible to have a good time at a party without alcohol, even if they do not drink themselves. Parents, schools, and communities have been trying for decades to reverse this perception but with little success. Perhaps adults have misunderstood the reason parties are so important to midadolescents.

I found it difficult to get students to open up and tell me about this aspect of their lives. Whenever I would venture here, it was tough to get students to move beyond sarcasm, humor, and even defensiveness. As a parent and youth worker, I had a concern for the students, but my "adult" status meant they didn't trust me when it came to this topic. Still, I was able to learn enough to achieve the following two insights.

The Importance of Community

In my effort to understand midadolescent partying, I soon realized that I needed to shift my focus from the alcohol (and marijuana) to the communal experience the teens were seeking to share. The important thing was the community, not the substances that were being used.

In listening to the stories surrounding the party world, I noticed that the tales had a common element. The experiences and antics of the players, not the alcohol, made the parties memorable. Stories create a collective narrative of past experience that points to both a shared memory (which creates unity and binds people together in a common history) and the promise of a bright future, based on the narrative of the past.

Parties are social gatherings that allow adolescents to participate in one of the most central and basic human experiences—community celebrations that remind people of their common past and guide them into the future. Parties are not about the party but about the longing for community.

The Use of Substances

Teens may gravitate toward alcohol and marijuana, but on a functional level, these substances are no different from any culture's symbols and sensory aids (from candles and incense to peyote and reserve vintage wine) that provide celebratory and ritualistic elements for a gathering. The substances aid in creating communal rituals and shared experiences.

Regrettably, in our culture, the use (and almost always the abuse) of alcohol and marijuana as a central feature of parties creates an artificial celebration. Many times I heard the old saying "The party begins when the beer shows up!" Here, beer is not just a "sensory aid" but an important symbol. The party starts when the beer shows up for both those who drink and those who don't.

Certainly substances like alcohol and marijuana enhance the stories adolescents tell later, stories of how someone got so drunk

168

Minor Fault

Young adults under twenty-one may not be able to buy alcohol. But they can get it easily enough. One in five adult men will buy it for them. So says a study out of the University of Minnesota's school of public health. The study said men were far more apt to buy minors alcohol than women, but only if they were asked outside a liquor store. Only 8 percent agreed if asked inside the store. Also booze buyers near urban liquor stores were more apt to buy than those loitering outside suburban stores.

he kissed the wrong date or threw up on the hall rug are pretty common. But such stories should not keep us from realizing that adolescents are also hungry for a transcendent experience that provides meaning, hope, adventure, and carefree celebration—a value that we adults have taught them all too well.

This may sound disturbing to some, especially to those who have a bias against the idea of the teenage party, but once we realize that parties are one of the few avenues adolescents have to find a sense of community, ritual, and celebration, we may have a greater understanding and compassion for this potentially negative event.

Parents and other adults who desire to protect and nurture midadolescents would do well to approach the issue of parties at the level of respect for the communal experience. The best way to cause a midadolescent to dive underground is to disparage uncaringly what is in many cases an important community ritual for their teens.

A Place "Where Everybody Knows Your Name"

The party ethic of the high school world, coupled with the centrality of alcohol as a staple of the experience, is commonplace today, and this has apparently been true for several decades. As I

Assessing Alcohol Use in Your Youth Group

Jeremy Zach

In *Hurt* I learned that if there is a group of students (a student cluster), there will be at least a few students (if not all) who are drinking. I realized that the desire to party goes beyond just getting drunk. "Drinking is not about drinking; it is about community." Adolescents see being in the party scene not only as a social ritual, but also as a place where they can be involved and accepted. At the core of every adolescent is the longing to belong.

The reality of the party scene was not surprising, but affirmed what I had read in *Hurt*. It would be silly to deny the research and not to address the reality of adolescents and alcohol. The abuse of alcohol is a difficult problem without a simple solution.

How did I address the alcohol situation in my high school ministry? Honestly addressing the alcohol problem in a youth ministry is a step-by-step process. There is no perfect program, no overnight fix, or insightful teaching that will automatically get adolescents to stop drinking. It is imperative to remember (although I forget a lot) the transformative power that the *Holy Spirit* brings, not the youth worker! I handled the alcohol situation with three different techniques.

First, I needed to assess the alcohol use in the high school ministry. I needed to know *when* the students were partying and *who* exactly was partying. I started by asking students a lot of questions, both individually and collectively. Oddly enough, my

indicated above, midadolescents feel a deep need for community, as does the rest of society. We saw this in the TV series *Cheers*, one of the most popular TV series of the 1980s and early 1990s. *Cheers* was set in a Boston bar, but the emphasis was not on booze; it was on community.

The only conclusion I came to from talking to kids about partying is that for the vast majority of adolescents, drinking is not about drinking; it is about community. What I observed was that almost every midadolescent either loves to party or affirms the ritual of the party and therefore wants to be involved, even if he or she does not drink.

Adolescents long for a place to belong. There is ample evidence across centuries and cultures that children become adults via a system of rituals that celebrate the society they are entering. Because

170

students did not have a problem sharing their alcohol experiences and party stories with me.

Also I spent time on their MySpace and Facebook pages. MySpace and Facebook are our friends! They give a firsthand perspective of what happens on Friday and Saturday nights. (At times I wonder if the kids add to the stories to glorify their alcohol consumption.) Through these websites I had access to the pictures, bulletins, and commentary that described the party from the night before.

For the last segment of my alcohol assessment, I took a survey, asking each student to answer questions anonymously (either in open-ended or multiple-choice format). Some of the questions were: *Where do you get alcohol? How many parties are there in a week? How much are you likely to drink at a party? Why do you drink? Do your friends drink?* After the assessment I realized that 65 percent of the kids in my group were partyers and they were partying on Friday and Saturday nights.

Second, I taught a series that I called "Realities of Our Identity." The goal was to communicate that who we are should not determine what we do to gain acceptance. We are the children of God; we already belong to the heavenly Father. My students need to put value on their identity in Christ, rather than putting value on the identity imposed on them from the party scene. It is my desire that these students be authentic in who they are as followers of Christ.

Third, our high school ministry team orchestrated a variety of weekend activities that encouraged interaction and connection between the many student clusters. It was clear to me that student clusters party because they love social interaction,

we have abandoned our young, we have effectively taken from them a formalized expression of communal celebration and left them to their own devices to celebrate the life they have.

Why is alcohol involved? All one has to do is glance at popular media, marketing strategies, and even adult behaviors to see why adolescents believe alcohol is necessary to experience community. We have taught our young that they need a mind-numbing substance to find the courage to relate to one another and we have created a structure in which we advertise their need for it and provide access to it.

Many midadolescents cannot articulate the reason they have a passion for parties or even their love for alcohol. But their behavior, humor, and social structure scream loudly that they cannot survive without a safe, welcoming place and a ritual.

171

connection, and excitement, and these gatherings gave the students these outlets— without the alcohol.

Also the students had a chance to spend time with adult leaders. It was important to find adults who genuinely cared about the students, with whom the students felt comfortable. My amazing adult leaders were willing to open up their homes and give their Friday and Saturday nights to be with the cluster to which they were connected. Whatever the clusters enjoyed doing, the adults would do it with them. For example, clusters could go paint balling, bowling, to the arcade, to a baseball game, to the movies, and so on. The intention of these weekend nights was to demonstrate what authentic, sober connection looks like (with their friends and other adults who care for them outside of the church).

Above all, there are no overnight remedies to the alcohol problem. The problem lies not with the alcohol alone, but with a genuine longing for community. Assess your students' alcohol consumption. Start by accepting where your students are and then lead them to where you would like them to be. Give them opportunities to find a place to belong apart from the party scene.

Remember that the change must move from the *inside out*. We have to trust that God is at work inside their hearts.

Jeremy Zach, a former aspiring pilot, surrendered to Christ in 2002 to follow his call as a youth pastor. He holds a communications degree from the University of Minnesota–Twin Cities and a master of divinity degree from Fuller Theological Seminary. Jeremy is the youth pastor at Church By The Sea in Laguna Beach, California, http://jeremyzach.blogspot.com.

Unfortunately, the world to which we have abandoned our kids provides this safety and ritual in environments that frequently include alcohol. Our challenge is to find other environments where our kids can experience community and ritual in ways that are meaningful to them.

helping our kids cope and grow

12

how adults can help our kids

In the movie *X-Men 2*, Jean Grey saves the day for her friends by using her mutant powers to hold up a crumbling dam, only to sacrifice herself in the process. As I watched the film, I could not help but think that the challenges Jean faced were no greater than those faced by adults who care about today's teens.

But a lone figure standing with hands upraised cannot alone halt our culture's shift toward systemic abandonment of our young. This does not mean, however, that we cannot soften its impact or compensate for its cruelty. We are not powerless. When we are willing to walk beside even one young person, we can make a difference.

Such individual attention is at odds with the mass nature of our culture. We have switched from focusing on individuals to focusing on the group, the crowd, the statistics, the record, the program, the institution.

It's clear that taking on teen abandonment will require an intense, lengthy, proactive struggle from every corner of society, but I have concluded that the best thing we can do is to address the needs of midadolescents one at a time at the point of the individual adolescent. Adults must care for and reach the individuals who have suffered from abandonment throughout their lives.

Our cultural ethos of bigger, faster, and splashier is bound to fail when we're trying to address a problem as broad and as deep as abandonment. Kids need adults who can "think small" and invest in the long-term work of deliberate, consistent, authentic, and nurturing concern and care. Systemic abandonment sounds like a vast problem, and it is. But one adult who is there for a young person can significantly address the feelings of abandonment he or she experiences. Our response must begin with an individual student who needs the encouragement and leadership of an adult who genuinely cares.

One of the main reasons for the retreat of adolescents from the adult world into the world beneath is that many adults have let them down throughout their lives. Most midadolescents carry with them a list of adults who did not protect or look out for them, whether it was a Sunday school teacher who kicked them out of class, a peewee soccer coach who angrily took them out of a game for making a mistake, or a teacher who called on them when they weren't prepared. These experiences become the source of a lack of trust in adults who say they care.

If adults are willing to wade through and wait out this lack of trust and honestly desire to come alongside and nurture adolescents as they make their way into the community of adults, it will not take long for adolescents to recognize the sincerity and allow these adults into their lives. The only qualification an adult needs is the willingness and fortitude to care authentically.

In the rest of this chapter I want to talk about the ten things we must do if we want to make a difference in the lives of young people.

1. Help Organizations and Programs Focus on Nurturing Youth

Once upon a time America was a nation of communities, starting on the neighborhood level, with families and individuals who lived near each other and actually knew each other. But that was then. Now we seem more like a nation of organizations, corporations, and bureaucracies.

Today kids from big cities and small towns need the same thing: a community of people, organizations, and institutions that have

Don't You Google Me, Young Man!

Parents say their children spend too much time in front of screens these days. Television is still the biggest bad influence, according to a recent study by the University of Southern California. Nearly half of all parents say their children watch too much of it. But the Internet is an up-and-coming ne'er-do-well, with 21 percent of parents saying their kids spend too much time online.

Parents often restrict access to both as forms of punishment: 57 percent of parents say they've withheld television privileges from their children, and 47 percent say they've cut their children's Internet access from time to time.

their individual needs and interests in mind. These new forms of community could take many forms:

- parents who band together to encourage youth sports leagues that allow all children to play the same amount and affirm all participants for their contribution
- schools that seek creative ways to reduce homework, while increasing test scores and student enthusiasm for learning
- communities that sponsor regular meetings at which all those who work with adolescents—school officials, sports and recreation leaders, parents, church leaders, employers, police, and social service workers—can come together to help one another assess their unique and collective efforts to care for each child and adolescent in the community

Some of us are affiliated with organizations or institutions that were founded to serve the needs of young people, but over time, organizational drift may have allowed a lack of focus on these founding principles. In such cases, we need to take back the original intent and design of nurturing opportunities and reshape how we serve the young in every community.

2. Provide Young People with a Stable, Secure, and Loving Presence

I remember talking to Sara, a young woman who was confident, proud, smart, and witty. Basically Sara told me I was crazy and that teens like her did not need well-meaning adults in their lives. But the more we talked, the more Sara softened up and changed her tune.

Sara's parents had struggled, and her father had left the family more than once. She felt she didn't have a safe place in the

Youth Culture Update

Ma, Can the Sony Sleep Over? Forever?

Who knew that the "HD" in HD-TV might stand for "health damage"? But when children share their rooms with a television set, that moniker might be all too close to the truth. According to a recent study, about 70 percent of third graders have TV sets in their bedrooms. That translates to a lot of heavy-duty screen time: Children who have their own televisions watch about thirty hours of TV a week—nine hours more than their less "networked" peers.

Common sense would suggest that so much *Gilligan's Island* ain't healthy for anybody, and researchers agree. On average, children with TVs in their bedrooms are less likely to read, exercise, or sleep sufficiently, and more likely to smoke, snack, and be overweight. Oh, and the TV kids scored lower on school tests too.

And once a child gets a TV in his or her room, it's about as hard to pry those stubborn sets out of there as it is to drag a food-aholic away from an all-you-can-eat buffet line.

"In our experience, it is often hard for parents to remove a television set from a child's bedroom," said researcher Leonard H. Epstein of the State University of New York at Buffalo.

world and believed there was nobody in her life who was truly concerned about her needs. She said she felt alone, stuck, ignored, and used.

Then Sara began telling me about the good old days of her childhood. She wept as she remembered the times when she sat on her father's lap watching television or went on long walks in the park with her mom and little sister. "But those days are long gone," she said, wiping her eyes. "You know it and I know it. I am on my own. I just can't let myself think this way. It's stupid to even think about. I can't take it. I've got to go."

Many midadolescents feel the same way, though the details of their individual stories are as varied as they can be. Some teens may seem impenetrable, callous, or independent, like Sara was at first. This is not a smokescreen. It is an authentic depiction of how they have chosen to cope with the dangers posed through being abandoned by those they had trusted.

Adults should not be fooled by such displays. And instead of retreating, we should reach out with consistent love and concern that constitute the only way of showing teens that someone really does care for them.

3. Build Authentic, Intimate Relationships with Teens

Every young person needs to know that at least one adult knows him or her well enough to know when there is a problem and be able to do whatever it takes to bring him or her into the community of healthy adulthood. For ages, such relationships were part of the job description of parents, but as we all know, not all teens are fortunate enough to have parents who really care and know how to express that care in ways that are relationally relevant.

Many parents are overburdened and at their wit's end about what to do with their kids. In our segmented, fragmented culture, neighbors seldom know one another's names. Teachers, even the best ones, get overwhelmed by the multifaceted demands of their jobs. Families are so busy that they don't have time for an evening meal together. In such circumstances, even the best parents find it difficult to meet all the nurturing requirements of today's postmodern adolescents.

179

Every child needs authentic, intimate relationships with adults until he or she has completed much of the adolescent process. Parents, teachers, or youth workers cannot do it alone. The only way to stem the tide of abandonment is for every caring adult to get involved in the life of one or more young people and encourage others to do the same.

Nothing else will make a difference—not more baseball fields, more programs and events, or more job opportunities. Because the root of the issues related to contemporary adolescence has to do with the adults who have left this age group, allowing them to flounder on their own, the answer is relationships with adults who sincerely care. That is the primary need of this abandoned generation.

4. Study Youth Culture

If you were going to work with a medical crew fighting AIDS in a foreign land, it would help if you understood something about the beliefs, customs, sexual practices, and medical knowledge of the people you hoped to serve. The same is true with young people. Teens inhabit their own world, and most of them consume tons of pop culture. While we don't need to know every detail about every celebrity, song, or website, it helps to have the attitude of a student who seeks continually to learn more about youth culture.

We've all seen fifty-something teachers or counselors who approach a group of kids and start their comments with the deadly words, "When I was in high school . . ." Such folks may mean well, but their positive impact on kids will be lessened if they are continually speaking to teens from behind their own historical filters.

Anyone who works directly with adolescents needs to be aware and even trained about the broad patterns of contemporary youth culture. There are formal ways of receiving such training. For example, Fuller Seminary, the school with which I am affiliated, now requires that all graduating students take one or more classes in "cultural literacy," no matter their degree path or career goals. Likewise, I think we all need to increase our cultural literacy through classes and seminars, publications like *Entertainment Weekly*, and websites that follow youth culture.

But the most important thing is not classes or magazines. The biggest thing is having the attitude of a learner. I always try to ask kids what music they are listening to or what movies they are seeing and what life messages or meaning they are getting out of the pop culture they consume.

5. Work with Others Who Serve Adolescents

None of us can turn the tide of adolescent abandonment on our own. Whether we work in a school, church, social services agency, sports league, or in a therapeutic capacity, we need the help of the other adults who impact the lives of the teens we serve.

It is typical of human nature that we build our own kingdoms and even compete with others for limited funds or volunteers. But if we are going to help today's teens, we need to be atypical. We need to reach out and work with other adults who have teens' best interests at heart.

I am well acquainted with the competitive infighting that characterizes many faith-based youth programs. I wrote about this

Youth Culture Update

Early to Bed

New research suggests that teens who sleep late on weekends may get something akin to jet lag, causing them to underperform academically.

The research, conducted on children ages fifteen and sixteen, shows that sleeping in on weekends causes the body's internal clock to reset itself—and a return to "normalcy" Monday morning can make the body rather cranky.

All that makes for a catch-22 for many teens, who rely on weekends to catch up on sleep. Some stay up late to do homework and wake up early to go to school. Most experts say teens should be getting around nine hours of sleep a night, even though most teens report getting just seven hours.

problem in my "Page One" column in the May/June 2008 issue of *YouthWorker Journal*:

> Funny thing, human nature. We plead with God that He will reach the kids in our church, our neighborhood, our school, our town.
>
> Then, an hour later at a local restaurant, we see a bunch of cool kids with a Young Life staffer, and we turn away in frustration.
>
> Or we notice a Baptist youth pastor leading a serious Bible study with his kids in the side room, and they are into it! Heck, the local Catholic priest has more kids hanging with him than you do!
>
> Fifteen minutes later one of our kids shows up for a meeting. But the first thing he says is, "My dad made me come."
>
> Is it any surprise we find ourselves praying, "Lord, when are You going to bless our ministry?"

Putting into Practice

Working Together to Overcome Abandonment

Ken Knipp

In all honesty, I felt discouraged after reading *Hurt*. I have spent thirty-five years in professional youth ministry of one form or another, and the reality of systemic abandonment is both real and daunting. I believe *Hurt* thoroughly *describes* the world as it is for a great majority of young people; however, *Hurt* does not *prescribe* responses for those of us who both care about young people and have committed ourselves to them and their future.

I have reflected at length on the question posed in chapter 12: "What do midadolescents need?" While I agree with Chap's comments that youth need (1) refocused, nurturing organizations and programs, (2) a stable and secure loving presence, and (3) authentic intimate relationships with adults, I have also tried to consider how those three needs can actually be met in practical ways. The reality is that for many young people, the organizations and programs that impact their lives are not necessarily nurturing. Many young people lack a stable and secure loving presence, whether that is in their family or elsewhere. Finally, too many young people have no authentic meaningful relationships with adults and, even for those who may have such a relationship, there ought to be multiple adult relationships to truly overcome the effects of systemic abandonment.

I am a parent of two married sons in their late twenties and also a seventeen-year-old daughter who is a junior in high school. I have frequent contact with both volunteers and paid staff who work with young people through Young Life. Also I am involved in a

Somehow we still are more committed to our thing than to what God is doing in and through others.

Does the competition I am describing sound familiar? You may not even work in a church setting, but the same kind of competitive spirit raises its head no matter where we serve.

In most communities, schools, youth centers, churches, youth sports leagues, and other youth-focused groups function independently of one another. For each adolescent in a given community to be cared for, regardless of talent, ability, or even attitude, programs with similar goals must work together.

Obstacles to networking range from a lack of time to a lack of awareness of what others are doing in a given community. Fre-

local congregation that does a fairly good job of youth ministry. As I write these words, I am very aware of two eighteen-year-olds who were in a tragic, single-car accident three nights ago. These two young men were driving at a high rate of speed, under the influence of alcohol, and they were not wearing seat belts when their vehicle left the road. One died at the scene and the other is in a coma with serious head injuries as of this writing. In my opinion, what has happened to these two young men is the unfortunate outcome of young people living too much of their lives in the "world beneath," not meaningfully involved in enough authentic relationships with adults or rooted in a stable and secure loving presence that provides both boundaries and identity.

In my opinion, the most helpful response to the needs of midadolescents is shaped by our responses to the following questions. I think these questions are fundamental whether one is a parent, teacher, youth worker, coach, therapist, or social worker.

Who specifically are the midadolescents in my world? For whom am I a significant person? The answer may be young people in my own family, my classroom, my youth group, or on an athletic team.

What other adults care about the young people in my world? That is, what adults care about the specific kids in my world, not young people in general? The answer to this question might include other family members, teachers, coaches, youth workers, or counselors.

How can I cooperate with the other people who care about the young people in my world? This requires initiative with other adults and probably means that we will be involved with a small number of young people.

quently people and organizations that serve the young feel overwhelmed by a lack of resources and the demands they face. What few seem to recognize is that a network of like-minded people and organizations creates a flow of additional resources and strategic opportunities. A seminar for parents, for example, would be expensive if a local PTA sponsored it independently. If a local community network, comprised of various agencies and organizations, hosted it, a better (and cheaper) parent seminar could be made available to all. Imagine what could happen if Little League sponsors, local schools, the police, the YMCA, and churches met together two or three times a year with the sole intent of addressing issues of abandonment in a community.

I have to say the most effective responses I have seen to the systemic abandonment of young people have been when parents were truly cooperating with teachers and/or youth workers and/or coaches to talk about the *specific needs* of *specific adolescents* in their world.

One of the primary points that Chap makes is that young people live much of their lives related to one or more clusters of friends. The most helpful responses I have seen to systemic abandonment are several adults (a couple of parents and a youth worker; a teacher, a parent, and a youth worker; a couple of youth workers and a coach) strategizing together on how they could respond to a specific cluster or clusters of young people. While the numbers of kids addressed is not very high, a few adults working together can actually make a real difference for more than a small number of clusters. This might mean influencing a coach to lower his or her time expectations of kids. It might mean a couple of parents agreeing to set a clear boundary on certain behaviors. It might mean a couple of parents and a youth worker agreeing on appropriate expectations of a youth ministry or program.

When this kind of collaboration takes place between a few people who truly care about adolescents, the results can be very encouraging. I have seen this happen in local Young Life ministries, in a local congregation, and in a community where parents really communicated with one another. It does not happen automatically; it takes communication, initiative, and persistence, but the results are definitely worth the effort.

Ken Knipp is currently Vice President of Training for Young Life and lives in Colorado Springs, Colorado. He has served as an Area Director for Young Life in central Indiana, as Regional Director for Young Life in Michigan, and has been in his current position since June 2006.

Sometimes there are issues of institutional or even personal mistrust that keep adults from working together to help the kids they serve. But such lack of collaboration comes with a high cost. The challenges are so great that we should lay down our petty jealousies or turf battles and work together for the good of our young people and the community.

6. Understand Kids and Provide Them with Boundaries

To nurture adolescents, we need to understand their changing world and provide boundaries so their choices have as few serious consequences as possible. What does it mean for adults to provide boundaries? It comes down to a commitment to a simple truth: the nurture and care of the young in society is the responsibility of every adult in society. Every adult who cares about the young must do whatever it takes to address and confront any other adult, organization, or policy that contributes to kids' abandonment. Small, relatively simple actions can make a huge difference over time. Consider:

- an assistant youth football coach who meets with the coaching staff and parents to discuss ways to encourage every player equally, regardless of experience, size, or talent
- a high school teacher who notices other teachers' disparaging comments toward students and makes sure the administration takes steps to address such flagrant violations of that profession's lofty calling
- a few parents who find out that a local merchant is selling chewing tobacco to football players and arrange a meeting with that merchant (and others in town), the city council, the school administration, and law enforcement to ensure that unsafe and addictive substances are not readily available to adolescents

These are merely a few examples that show how a caring community of adults can provide boundaries for the young in a given community. Think of additional things you can do in your own community.

185

7. Equip and Encourage Parents to Help Today's Adolescents

Many parents feel like members of a poorly trained rescue squad at a burning building. They are aware that youth culture has changed in significant ways and they want to do what they can, but some are so panicked they run around causing more commotion than calm.

Parents need to know that what is happening in today's world is not their fault and that with some work and understanding they can build good and productive relationships with their children, even in the midst of cultural chaos.

Parents don't need to know everything about contemporary youth culture but they do need to grasp these three key things we have discussed in this book:

- the reality of lengthened adolescence
- the phenomenon of layered and underground living
- the perception of adolescents that they are on their own and must figure out how to live

If parents (including stepparents and guardians) recognize and understand these aspects of adolescence, they will be well on their way to parenting with a certain level of confidence.

8. Make Sure Teens Have Adult Advocates Who Know and Care for Them

A popular myth that many of us have grown up with is the idea that young people need the influence of a single, positive role model. This myth has been perpetuated by otherwise outstanding programs such as Big Brothers and Big Sisters as well as worthwhile programs that focus on finding struggling kids a mentor to help them whenever they are in need.

Unfortunately, a single individual does not have the ability to be present in the variety of ways an adolescent needs. In our culture, the diversity of demands is simply too great for any one individual to address. Plus, even the best mentors eventually leave, which in some ways can be worse than if they were never there in the first

Not Leaving the Kids to Kids

Jim Candy

Outsourcing isn't just a term reserved for the business world. When it comes to youth ministry, our church had been in the outsourcing business for years. Over our church's history of youth ministry, a subtle mentality had emerged. Youth ministry was exclusively the job of college students. We had *outsourced* the "job" of reaching kids to these young, energetic people who could "handle" them. It wasn't just the congregation that thought college students were the only youth workers in the church—it was also the paid staff in the youth ministry (myself included).

Reading *Hurt* lifted a veil from our eyes. With the nature of extended adolescence, we essentially had a ministry of adolescents leading adolescents. Actually it was worse than that. Most of our paid youth staff were in their mid-twenties. We had late adolescents (paid staff), leading middle adolescents (volunteers), leading early adolescents (kids). In that sense, we had no adults involved in the ministry.

If the church should be a place where kids are folded into the whole congregation like a caring family, we were failing. It hurt to admit that kids needed more than we were offering. We asked God for a shift—dreaming of a team split evenly between college students and older adults.

A few pioneering adults joined our team. Eric, an attorney in his mid-forties, developed a friendship with John, an energetic eighth grader. When life turned complicated for John in high school, he did not turn to his college leaders. He went to Eric. Eric was surprised John chose him—he had often felt awkward around John and his friends but, for John, *Eric was safe.*

place. To a needy child or adolescent, the failed promise of intimate companionship and nurture is devastating.

Everything I have ever read about helping kids has shown that *several* positive and supportive relationships that offer kids the same messages will have a greater effect on the life of a young person than any individual person. One fan, even if he or she is a great one, is not enough.

Every adult must attempt to add to the cumulative message of protection, nurture, warmth, and affection being delivered to kids. It takes several if not dozens of consistently supportive and encouraging messages to counteract the effects of systemic aban-

Reshaping our leadership team was important, but *Hurt* showed us even this change fell short. Merely involving older adults in youth ministry is shortsighted and even a little arrogant—as if the key to faith in kids is how cleverly we structure our leadership team! No, we needed to think more broadly. How could we create an environment where kids had a network of caring adults that *transcended* the youth ministry?

A major philosophical shift followed. We began to see ourselves as "relational brokers." We needed to empower adults to build meaningful relationships with kids, even if these adults never spent one minute as a part of our "programmed" time.

We urged parents to create a network of five other adults who would genuinely love and influence their kids. We shared this dream tirelessly, and a funny thing happened—*parents started doing it*. We had become their partners. We also started spending time with teachers, coaches, pediatricians—whoever crossed paths with kids in their everyday lives. How could the youth ministry encourage more adults to genuinely love kids?

This is a work in progress. Actually this work will always be in progress. There is no "arrival point." Results are hard to measure—but great stories, like Eric and John, have emerged. *Hurt* shifted more than our theory about kids; it reshaped dramatically our practice of who builds relationships with kids and how.

Jim Candy is a twelve-year youth and family ministry veteran, including ten years as Director of Middle School Ministries at First Presbyterian Church in Boulder, Colorado. Now he serves at Menlo Park Presbyterian Church in California. He is a frequent contributor to youth ministry periodicals as well as a popular speaker.

donment. By far the best way to help our young is by being a chorus of support and a choir of commitment.

9. Youth Ministers Need to Rethink Their Methods

In much of this book I have been addressing any and all adults who work with kids as parents, teachers, social workers, or counselors. Now I would like to share a few words with my friends in Christian youth work.

Youth ministry, when done well, is both encouraging and generally effective at giving kids a sense of a caring and principled adult community. And the people who work in youth ministry are for the most part sincere, well-intentioned adults who want to see those under their care come to a personal relationship with Christ and have this faith experience become a growing reality in the kids' lives.

So far, so good. But there is an aspect of youth ministry that concerns me. In some churches and communities, youth work is becoming increasingly institutionalized and programmatic. To the degree youth programs do this, they are inviting young people's disinterest or outright disdain.

Of course an adult who is more interested in the welfare of individual teens than in the program will have a better chance of retaining the loyalty and interest of students throughout midadolescence. But often the demands and expectations of executing a program become the central driving focus. It takes little for a midadolescent to feel as though the program matters more than he or she does. This creates a crisis in youth ministry. Once students begin to see youth ministry in the same light as other institutions that have abandoned them, youth workers have lost a crucial link.

I have seen hundreds of youth ministry programs, consulted with several dozen churches and parachurch groups, and interacted with thousands of youth ministry leaders and students over the course of my life. Here's something I have learned: abandonment is not limited to "secular" programs and institutions but is alive and well in the systems and structures of the church. Youth ministry is often concerned with numerical growth, superficial and instant response, and active attendance, making it more about the ministry than about the individuals. This is a recipe for abandonment.

For example, what happens when twelve students arrive at a youth group when the leader expected a group of eighteen? The first question from the leader is, "Where is everybody?" This prompts the twelve who *are* there to wonder if their presence matters at all.

In addition, some adults have used the idea that "only students can reach students" as an excuse for avoiding one-on-one relationships with individual teens. Adolescents are desperate for adults who care enough to guide them gently and patiently into adulthood. When adults say, "Only students can reach students," teens hear them saying something different. They hear abandonment. They

Creating a Culture of Safety

Wendell Loewen

In the last few years I've come to the conclusion that adolescents see most youth ministry programs as hostile adult systems.

I remember when a speaker at a national youth event invited students to recommit to Christ, a unified, almost choreographed wave of teens rose to their feet. I couldn't find one student still seated. Was this a survival act in a hostile environment? Students calculated expectations and did the safest thing. I've witnessed this phenomenon too many times.

But I see this every week in youth group too, so I strive to create a culture of safety to counter teen assumptions of hostility. This comes by doing the little things, persistently over the long haul. Here are some ideas.

Utilize lots of accepting adults. Adult convergence means adolescents must interact with a wider range of caring, accepting adults. Warm smiles and gentle hugs can disarm their assumptions about a hostile adult world. With a growing sense of acceptance, teens grant us a measure of trust.

hear adults saying, "I do not have the time or the ability to reach out to you or your world."

Students should be encouraged to be involved in ministry in ways that allow them to explore their calling and giftedness. My concern comes when we expect students to lead and run a program without the careful, strategic, and deliberate investment of adults whose task it is to lead students to maturity and assimilation.

10. Youth Ministers Need to Rethink Youth Ministry Goals

For many years I defined the goal of youth ministry as encouraging students to develop a personal, authentic faith in Christ. I still see that as a crucial piece of the puzzle, but it's not the whole picture. An overemphasis on "individualized" salvation plays into the individualism of our culture and neglects teens' need to be a part of a vital and vibrant community.

God calls people to become members of communities of faith. The message of reconciliation with God is an invitation to join

Cluster your small groups. Breaking up clusters is counterproductive and antagonistic, so structure your small groups around natural cluster formations and let them function as adolescent systems. As a small-group leader, I want to let go of the wheel and operate like a coach, letting my students provide more of the group's content and direction.

Swap stories. Sharing and hearing stories can create powerful relational bonds. Adults internalize today's teenage stresses, and students discover they share things in common with adults. Try having students and volunteers answer the question: "How did you get in trouble as a kid?" You'll experience laughter and new levels of trust.

Relax a little. My adult agenda demands 100 percent student participation. If I push it, youth group becomes about the adults in charge—it's no longer safe. Some nights hurting teens don't feel like doing the egg-in-the-armpit relay. Some activities only magnify their insecurities. If kids don't want to share prayer concerns—it's okay to pass. I want to communicate that their stresses are valid. I won't coerce them—it's unsafe.

with others who recognize their individual and collective need to love God and to live in love with one another. That's why I have refined my definition of the goal of youth ministry as follows: *The goal of youth ministry should be to make disciples of Jesus Christ who are authentically walking with God within the context of intimate Christian community.*

Midadolescent faith development is a long and difficult journey that is best taken with others who are on the same road to God. Those who approach discipleship as Lone Rangers are bound to fail.

The process of helping an adolescent develop a consistent faith takes time, patience, and perseverance from loving and caring adults in the Christian community. Faith is a long, complex journey, and adolescents need someone who will walk alongside them as long as it takes.

Ultimately, the goal of youth ministry is not about helping to shape a personal faith. The goal is the full relational and systemic assimilation of the emerging adult into the life of the Christian

Encourage disagreement. One night while focusing on the fleeting value of posses-sions, Becca blurted, "But I like stuff." What a beautiful interruption! I stopped to praise Becca for her honesty—admitting I liked stuff too. Kids need to know that youth group is a safe place to express opinions and ask hard questions.

Be real about life. When we tell teens things like, "There are three keys to successful Christian living," we're lying. Life's just not that easy. So I carefully explore life's tensions—steering clear of pat answers. I can model what it means to follow Jesus in the midst of real life. Students identify with that.

It takes time and intentionality to create a culture of safety and build student trust. It's hard work and all your adult volunteers must be on board. But as the culture grows, you'll find that your youth ministry will become much deeper, more real, and more effective than you ever imagined.

Wendell Loewen is Associate Professor of Youth, Church, and Culture at Tabor College in Hillsboro, Kan-sas. He's a twenty-year youth ministry veteran who's been teaching youth ministry since 1997 and still volunteers with youth in his home church. He earned a doctor of ministry degree from Fuller Theological Seminary in 2005 and recently published *Beyond Me: Grounding Youth Ministry in God's Story* (Herald Press, 2008).

community known as the church. In a culture in which the young have been set adrift without a structure designed to invite them back into the core of adult life, the church must be different.

Those who would minister to today's adolescents must be com-mitted to reconnecting the young to the collective faith community. That means we must not only proclaim the doctrines of our faith but also roll up our sleeves, go to adolescents, listen to them, and unconditionally care for them.

My hope is that no matter where you serve, you will become one of the adults who surround young people in your community with a circle of committed and caring adults.

conclusion

the adventure continues

As I said in the introduction, my journey into the world of today's teens has been a real adventure, and I wouldn't exchange it for the world.

Over the past five years I've had plenty of opportunities to talk to other people about their thoughts on today's teens and teen culture. After hundreds of such discussions I've reflected again on some of the things I first said in *Hurt*. Here's what that reflection has shown me.

Lessons Learned

Even More So!

People ask me if I think things are getting better for today's teens. I wish I did, but in the last five years, I believe things have grown worse. Everybody agrees today's teens are in a heap of trouble, but few are doing anything about it. It's been a decade since the killings at Columbine High School in Denver, and have we changed the factors that cause kids to kill kids? No. Instead, such killings have become nearly routine.

There Is Hope

Yet all is not lost. One of the responses I got from readers was that *Hurt* was a real downer. I think that's a valid criticism and I

193

Youth of a Nation

Though many studies suggest that today's youth are out of step with the morals of their parents—they're more sexually promiscuous, for instance, and more apt to cheat and think it's okay—some Christian speakers suggest that they're also hungry for a deep, sincere relationship with God.

"I've discovered that this generation of young men and women is crying out for revival," wrote Becky Tirabassi, founder of Burning Hearts, Inc. Tirabassi regularly visits college campuses and Christian youth events, and she's seen youth attending in amazing numbers. More than seventy thousand youth attended an event named "The Call" in Nashville last July. At Northwestern College in St. Paul, Minnesota, four hundred students showed up for a four-hour prayer vigil. After the four hours was finished, many left the prayer room in tears.

The biggest problem these kids have, according to Tirabassi, is they don't have mentors to adequately shepherd and mentor them.

"I've been to dozens of campuses in the past three years and seen that the younger generation has started what [Charles] Finney called 'a new beginning of obedience to God,'" Tirabassi writes. "Is my generation ready to join them?"

have tried to address it by asking people who are making a difference in the lives of our young people to contribute to this book. Their comments appear in the sidebars of the chapters.

Looking at the big picture, I see darkness on the horizon. Our culture is broken, and we are passing this broken culture on to a new generation of young people.

On the other hand, when I look around, I see amazing people doing amazing things to reach out to kids in need. In *Hurt* I did not do a very good job of acknowledging these people and efforts. I was so focused on cultural analysis that I failed to praise individuals who were going against the grain. I am thankful that many of those people whom I asked to contribute to this book graciously agreed to do so.

Some revolutions start from the ground and move upward, and I believe that's what's happening with the problems facing today's teens. I hope you will find inspiration and encouragement from the examples you read in this book.

It's All About Abandonment

I'm sorry for using the "A" word again, but I must. In *Hurt* I identified abandonment as the primary reality shaping the lives of today's teens. In the last five years I've had plenty of time to assess whether I was accurate or off course. At the risk of appearing to pat myself on the back, I think I hit the nail on the head.

The more I talk to teens, hang out with their parents, or examine the mixed messages of our culture, the more convinced I become that many folks have washed their hands of the centuries-old obligation to care for and mentor our young until they can make the transition to the adult world.

Is abandonment the only issue teens face? No. But it's the central issue, and combating it should be our central focus.

Layers Reconsidered

In chapter 3 I say: "It is helpful to think of adolescents' social lives as made of layers of relationships, or even a variety of roles or personas that they adopt." I stand behind this statement, but at the same time I believe we need to do some more research and reflecting on the true nature of teens' emotional lives and the "world beneath" in which many of them live.

Perhaps over the next five years some of you can help me come to a better understanding of this phenomenon. I look forward to hearing your thoughts.

Kids Are Naively Optimistic, and I Love 'Em!

The majority of kids I have met believe in their hearts that some caring adult will eventually come alongside them and give them the love, guidance, and boundaries they desperately need. I hope they are right, and if everyone reading this book becomes one of these adults, we are moving in the right direction toward realizing this dream.

Of course my "cultural analyst" side says that many of these teens will be disappointed. I question whether there are enough caring adults to meet the demand. But for those kids who grow up wondering who is truly there for them, or kids who do not have the advantage of concerned and lovingly focused parents, coaches, teachers, and youth workers, the resultant feelings of inadequacy and isolation can impact them for years to come. We all have a lot to do to bring adults and adult systems and structures back into alignment with the developmental and cultural needs of kids.

I don't always feel kids innate optimism is well grounded but I love it. In part because of their hope, I will continue hanging around with kids and loving every minute of it!

Youth Culture Update

News Flash: Teens More Immature than Adults

New research confirms that teens don't think through their actions as well as adults—research that's encouraging lawmakers to reshape the rules that treat teens like adults when it comes to serious crime.

Overall, youth ages sixteen or seventeen are typically more impulsive, aggressive, vulnerable to peer pressure, and likely to take risks than adults are.

"It doesn't mean adolescents can't make a rational decision or appreciate the difference between right and wrong," said Dr. David Fassler, a psychiatry professor at the University of Vermont College of Medicine. "It does mean, particularly when confronted with stressful or emotional decisions, they are more likely to act impulsively, on instinct, without fully understanding or analyzing the consequences of their actions."

From My Journey to Yours

I've been working with adolescents for more than three decades in a variety of church, parachurch, school, and social service settings. But there's one sixteen-year-old girl I'll never forget. She came up to me after a presentation I had given on the subject of trust.

"I'll tell you why I don't trust anybody at this school or my parents," she told me. "Everybody is out for themselves. Teachers, coaches, parents, even my church group leaders—they are all out for themselves. Nobody gives a [expletive] about me! Nobody!"

In writing *Hurt* I examined tons of research and wrote about many of the kids I met, but it was voices like that of this young woman that stuck in my mind and made me change my life. When I completed *Hurt*, I made the commitment to begin spending a few hours a week as a volunteer with youth in my area through an organization called Young Life. I felt called to do this. I also felt I needed to keep myself from being a complete hypocrite. After all, how could I tell other people to get personally involved in the lives of kids unless I was willing to do so myself?

So in September 2002 I reached out to three junior football players and started having dinner with them every Monday night. It has been taxing, tiring, and downright hard at times, but I have fallen in love with Daniel, Nigel, and John. They have changed me, and my dream is that showing unconditional tenderness toward them has had an impact on their feelings of abandonment.

But enough about me. What about you? What will you do with the information, insights, and feelings you have encountered as you've read this book? Reading is a dangerous activity, and my hope and prayer are that something in this book moves you to action, whether it came from me, some of the experts who contributed their insights, or some of the young people who let me put them under the microscope. I'm not asking you to change the world. I'm just asking you to sacrifice a few hours a week to change the life of one teen.

As you think about this challenge, I want you to hear the words of a young man named Don, who was one of the students I met on my journey. Don gave me these words and asked me to put them in my book:

Sometimes, I'm not who I seem to be
Sometimes, I keep it all inside of me
I know I could use a friend
But how can I tell you what's in my head?

That's when I cry
I let the tears run down my face
In the darkness
Where you can't see me
And you can't ask me why.

But when you're there
I keep my head held high
With a smile upon my face
So you don't know my pain or what I'm going through.

It's too late, you can't help me now
It's too late, you can't help me now.

Is it really too late for Don? I don't think so. Nor is it too late for you and the young people in your world.

acknowledgments

First, I would like to thank Robert Hosack, my editor at Baker. Without him this book would not exist!

I also want to thank the people who helped me transform *Hurt* into *When Kids Hurt*. Steve Rabey, my coeditor at *YouthWorker Journal*, was instrumental in the process, as were these skilled wordsmiths: Lois Rabey and Monte Unger (editing); Paul Asay (editing and Youth Culture Update sidebars), and Cheri Gillard (who assembled and edited the Putting into Practice sidebars).

Thank you also to Dee, Chap, and Rob. From you I continue to learn what it means to be a man, a husband, a father, and a friend.

And a special word for Katie, my daughter, whose courage and honesty became the catalyst for a most amazing experience. She helped me learn what it means to take risks when it is right and to value a child over a career, growth over performance, and the "journey" over the "right now." Yes, each member of my family has been a master teacher, but for how Katie led us all into uncharted waters through her faithfulness and firm conviction, I will always be especially grateful.

And my heartfelt thanks go out to the twenty-some experts who shared their wisdom by writing the Putting into Practice sidebars. Their essays, which are born of hands-on experience, will help the readers grapple with the important issues we have addressed.

Many people helped me create *Hurt*. Amy Jacober and Mark Maines were especially helpful with the original research. Also Emrys, Jim, and Margaret worked many long hours and gave invaluable insight into refining this book. Where this book makes sense and works, much of the credit goes to these friends. If there are any errors, omissions, or even a leap or two in logic, the blame goes solely to me.

I was greatly helped by the administration, faculty, and staff at Crescenta Valley High School. I am fully aware that this is one of the best schools in the country, and to be embraced for my work among you was a true gift.

I especially want to thank high school students, both at Crescenta Valley and around the United States. Your openness and gut-wrenching honesty made this far more than a study or even a book. You changed me. I will never again be able to lump high school students into a huge, stereotypical mass, because now I see every one as a unique, valuable person who matters. Thank you, each one of you, for allowing me to see inside your world. I only hope I did you justice in this work.

Along with students, former students, friends, and colleagues around the world, I have continued to follow up on the original Hurt research. We learn something new every day. The book you hold in your hands is part of an ongoing attempt to tell the world what kids have revealed to us. Therefore, I dedicate this book to all those who study, walk with, and nurture young people. And please know that your emails, letters, phone calls, coffee conversations, articles, and books continue to influence and shape how I understand this generation.

Finally, I want to thank my students and colleagues at Fuller Theological Seminary. You teach me to keep pushing the envelope regarding what it means to care for those we are called to serve. May this project cause the world to be stirred to the point of taking our young seriously, and may it begin with us.

sources cited

Anderman, Eric M., Tripp Griesinger, and Gloria Westerfield. "Motivation and Cheating during Early Adolescence." *Journal of Educational Psychology* 90 (1998): 84–93.

Augustine, Saint. *Confessions.* Translated by Rex Warner. New York: Signet Classic, 2001.

Boyle, T. C. *Drop City.* New York: Penguin, 2004.

Brooks, David. "Making It: Love and Success at America's Finest Universities." no. 15, *Weekly Standard* 8, at www.weeklystandard.com/Content/Public/Articles/000/000/002/017ickdp.asp.

Clark, Chap. "Page One." *YouthWorker Journal,* May/June 2008.

Clark, Chap. *Hurt: Inside the World of Today's Teenagers.* Grand Rapids: Baker, 2004.

Curry, Erin. "American Youth More Conservative but Less Moral, Studies Report," at www.bpnews.net/bpnews.asp?ID=14511.

Duncan, Greg J, Johanne Boisjoly, and Kathleen Mullan Harris. "Sibling, Peer, Neighbor, and Schoolmate Correlations as Indicators of the Importance of Context for Adolescent Development." *Demography* 38, no. 3 (August 2001).

Elkind, David. *The Hurried Child: Growing Up Too Fast Too Soon.* 3rd ed. Cambridge, MA: Perseus Publishing, 2001.

———. *A Sympathetic Understanding of the Child: Birth to Sixteen.* Needham Heights, MA: Allyn and Bacon, 1994.

————. *Ties That Stress: The New Family Imbalance.* Cambridge, MA: Harvard University Press, 1994.

Harter, Susan, S. Bresnick, H. A. Boushey, and N. R. Whitesell. "The Complexity of the Self in Adolescence" in *Readings on Adolescence and Emerging Adulthood,* ed. Jeffrey J. Arnett. Upper Saddle River, NJ: Prentice-Hall, 2002.

Hersch, Patricia. *A Tribe Apart: A Journey into the Heart of American Adolescents.* New York: Ballantine, 1998.

Josephson Institute of Ethics. "Survey Documents Decade of Moral Deterioration: Kids Are More Likely to Cheat, Steal, and Lie than Kids Ten Years Ago," at www.josephsoninstitute.org/Survey2002/survey2002–pressrelease.htm.

Kerber, August. *Quotable Quotes on Education.* Detroit: Wayne State University Press, 1968.

Knox, David, Marty E. Zusman, and Kristen McGinty. "Deception of Parents during Adolescence." *Adolescence* 36 (Fall 2001).

Levine, Mel. *A Mind at a Time.* New York: Simon & Schuster, 2003.

Mahedy, William, and Janet Bernardi. *A Generation Alone: Xers Making a Place in the World.* Downers Grove, IL: InterVarsity, 1994.

McCabe, Donald Lee. "Academic Dishonesty among High School Students." *Adolescence* 34 (Winter 1999).

Melnick, Merrill J., Kathleen E. Miller, and Donald F. Sabo. "Tobacco Use among High School Athletes and Nonathletes: Results of the 1997 Youth Risk Behavior Survey." *Adolescence* 36 (Winter 2001).

Pipher, Mary. *Reviving Ophelia: Saving the Selves of Adolescent Girls.* New York: Ballantine, 1994.

Pope, Denise Clark. *Doing School: How We are Creating a Generation of Stressed Out, Materialistic, and Miseducated Students.* New Haven: Yale University Press, 2001.

Posterski, Donald C. *Friendship: A Window on Ministry to Youth.* Scarborough, Ont.: Project Teen Canada, 1985.

Powers, Ron. "The Apocalypse of Adolescence." *Atlantic* (March 2002), at http://www.theatlantic.com/doc/200203/powers.

Putnam, Robert D. *Bowling Alone: The Collapse and Revival of American Community.* New York: Simon & Schuster, 2000. To access the data used in *Bowling Alone,* go to www.bowlingalone.com/socialcapital.php3.

Rice, Anne. *Belinda.* New York: Berkley Trade, 2000.

Santrock, John W. *Adolescence.* 8th ed. New York: McGraw-Hill, 2001.

Solarz, Andrea. *American Psychological Association Healthy Adolescents Project: Adolescent Development Project.* Washington, D.C.: American Psychological Association, 2002.

Underwood, John. "A Game Plan for America." *Sports Illustrated,* February 23, 1981.

Wolff, Alexander. "The High School Athlete." *Sports Illustrated,* November 18, 2002.

Chap and others can speak to your group!

Chap Clark has written, co-written, or edited more than fifteen books, including *Hurt: Inside the World of Today's Teenagers*, *Disconnected: Parenting Teens in a MySpace World* (written with Dee Clark), *Daughters and Dads*, and *From Father to Son*.

Chap and other members of his ParenTeen seminars event team are available for speaking and consulting regarding the issues presented in this book. For information, visit the ParenTeen website: www.parenteen.com.

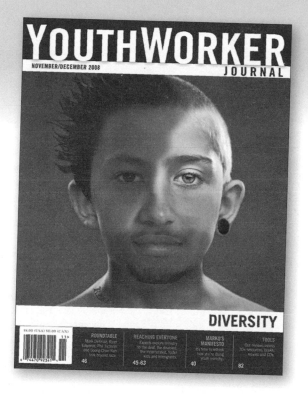

A Practical Guide for Parents

Guiding Your Kids Through the Critical Years

DISCONNECTED

Parenting Teens in
a MySpace® World

CHAP CLARK + DEE CLARK

Parents worry they don't have the understanding or training to be able to care for their kids in a world that is increasingly superficial, politicized, and performance driven. *Disconnected* makes the concepts and strategies described in the bestselling *Hurt: Inside the World of Today's Teenagers* accessible to parents. Due to the overwhelming response to *Hurt*, authors Chap and Dee Clark equip parents with an up-to-date, realistic parenting book that doesn't ignore the harsh realities of adolescent life. It builds a foundation for parents by describing exactly how things have changed, takes them through the various developmental stages their children go through, and gives them workable paradigms for parenting.

"No one writes more authentically, insightfully, realistically, hopefully, and readably than Chap and Dee about the vital topic of parenting. They 'get' teens and understand what it takes to reach them. No Pollyanna here. No formulas. Just hard-won, practical wisdom. Parents will find real help in these pages."

—**Dr. Larry Crabb**, founder and director, New Way Ministries

BakerBooks
a division of Baker Publishing Group
www.BakerBooks.com

Award-Winning Resource on Teens

"This book does a great job of framing the issues affecting adolescents. It provided me with some powerful insights. No wonder adolescents identify with the movies I have been making—the characters are on the same journey of trying to find hope and authenticity. This book is a great look inside the adolescent world, the world beneath the one exposed to adults."

—**Ralph Winter**, producer of *Star Trek IV* and *VI* and *X-Men*

What do teenagers really think about adults? If you think you know the answer, you may be in for a surprise. According to Chap Clark, today's adolescents have largely been abandoned by adults and left to fend for themselves in an uncertain world. As a result, teens have created their own world to serve as a shield against uncaring adults.

Based on six months of participant-observer research at a California public school, this book offers a somewhat troubling but insightful snapshot of adolescent life. It will surprise and enlighten parents, youth workers, counselors, pastors, and all who want to better understand the hearts and minds of America's adolescents.

BakerBooks

a division of Baker Publishing Group

www.BakerBooks.com